LADIES LAZARUS

LADIES LAZARUS

essays

PIPER J. DANIELS

TARPAULIN SKY PRESS
CA ∴ CO ∴ NY ∴ VT
2018

Ladies Lazarus
© 2018 Piper J. Daniels
ISBN-13: 9781939460134
Printed and bound in the USA

Tarpaulin Sky Press
P.O. Box 189
Grafton, Vermont 05146
www.tarpaulinsky.com

For more information on Tarpaulin Sky Press trade paperback and hand-bound editions, as well as information regarding distribution, personal orders, and catalogue requests, please visit our website at tarpaulinsky.com.

For Eddy Charles, Nancy Kaye, and Sarah Jade Daniels:
My North, my South, my East and West

CONTENTS

We have not touched the stars,
nor are we forgiven, which brings us back
to the hero's shoulders and the gentleness that comes,
not from the absence of violence, but despite
the abundance of it.

> — Richard Siken, "Snow and Dirty Rain"

Great untapped mercies live within us.

> — Elizabeth J. Colen, "Aposematic"

SIRENS

In the beginning, there is no way to assess, or even to imagine, the danger. Suicide, like many flirtations, starts with something small.

Smoking a cigarette.

Leaving something electric too close to the tub.

Knowing your seatbelt is unbuckled and leaving it that way.

And because modern life provides each of us with the sneaking suspicion that our existence is one of Sisyphus on speed, there is a freedom these small acts of defiance afford us, pressures they relieve, these subtle ways of leaning into and then whispering to death, *you don't have the nerve.*

The truth is, it is a shorter distance than you think from recklessness to despair. And because death, as a solution, is so all encompassing, so finite, other ways of coping pale in comparison. In no time, your neural pathways form a perfect arrow leading to the afterlife.

You wake up one morning, and you're not daring death anymore. In fact, death is daring you. Pointing out, for instance, how when the sun is right, the Golden Gate Bridge makes a black X upon the water. Marking the spot.

When all usefulness is over, when one is assured of an unavoidable and **imminent** death, it is the simplest of **human** rights to choose a quick and easy death in place of a slow and **horrible one**.

—Charlotte Perkins Gilman

You begin dreaming of the water, bean-green over blue.[1] And each night your body jerks awake as it mimics the motion of falling.

The choicest place from which to jump is light pole sixty-nine, facing the bay.

The time from the bridge to the water is four to seven seconds, depending upon the body's mass and the rate of acceleration.

The body falls at seventy-five miles per hour and kills ninety-eight percent of people on impact.

And this is why, for those of us who wish to go gently, the Bridge is such a meaningful place.

There will be, at most, a bit of blood in the water. No one needs to cut you down, looking into your blue face framed by the rope that hung you, nor does anyone need to scrub away the sunburst pattern your brain might make upon a wall.

Situated between the Nanjing Yangtze River Bridge in China and the Aokigahara forest in Japan, the Golden Gate Bridge is the second most popular place in the world to suicide. And once you're numb to everything but the possibility of jumping, you can find a strange if unexpected beauty in that.

---

1 Sylvia Plath

6

Goodbye, my friend, goodbye
My love, you are in my heart.
It was **preordained** we should part
And be reunited by and by.
Goodbye: no handshake **to endure**.
Let's have no **sadness**—furrowed brow.
There's nothing new in dying now
Though living is no newer.

—Sergei Esenin

Thoughts of death entered me through the Trojan horse of manic-depression, which presented itself when I was thirteen. I did not suspect, at that graceless age, that my demons and what I did with them differed so much from anyone else's.

Mental illness, in my case, began with cutting. It wasn't something I learned to do. It was something that rose up out of me, as though just beneath the skin a crucial text was making its way to the surface and in order to read it, I had to trace it from the outside. Avid reader that I was, the scars soon zebra-ed across my body.

Sometimes I cut a word: *help*. Sometimes a star, which amassed over time into a perfect Milky Way where my thighs met. Sometimes I carved a person's name, not to show them, never to show them, but because I needed to balance the weight of my love corporeally, to harvest and name the names of my heart. Or, in the case of people I hated, to draw names to the surface like a thin splinter.

I believed then that blood was the language of god, the surest way to catch his ear. These were the things I was thinking and feeling as an eighth grader. And when in the school year it was time for short sleeves, I discovered just how different, how deviant, I was. My carved arms became a juicy story disseminated by everyone in school. It would be the first time I was truly seen as a freak. To this day I have not learned to embrace my scars. Though at the time of this essay I have not cut in two years, I wear with shame my own scarred evidence. When asked about any particular maculation, I do not answer. I do not give ammunition. I will myself into a mental state in which I become silence itself.

When I am dead, and over me **bright April**
Shakes out her rain drenched hair,
Tho you should lean **above me** broken hearted,
I shall not care.
For I shall have peace.
As leafy trees are peaceful
When rain bends down the bough.
And I shall **be** more **silent** and cold hearted
Than you are **now**.

—Sarah Teasdale

Because the mind is so labyrinthine and psychology so uncertain, it makes sense to talk instead about the body as an instrument of manic-depression.

The way I presented—cutting, burning, swallowing glass—these were considered acts of self-injury, when in fact, I was trying to save myself by driving out the poltergeist who suddenly lived inside and spoke to me at night of unspeakable things. It is confusing the first time your body becomes an instrument of psychosis. There is no precedent for questioning or rejecting your senses. You hear a voice and have no way of knowing it's coming from inside the house.

Then there is the case of the body as an instrument of mania. I awoke one night from a dead sleep and a too-bright light was humming inside me. I didn't sleep for the next fourteen nights. Money moved easily through my fingers. I stole things for the pleasure of doing it. I allowed anyone inside who wanted me, and I lived through them, the etymology of ecstasy from the Latin *ekstasis*, "standing outside oneself." But every mouth that moved over me made a fissure, and I started cracking from the outside, bleeding light. And suddenly the world was slow and ink-black, and I realized the way I was sharing my body was not beautiful, but rather an invitation addressed to the brutal and the opportunistic. From that moment on, I lived in my body like a frightened child tormented by dark and darkness both. This was the body as an instrument of depression.

And so the body becomes a pale coin, depressed or manic, depending upon how the mind lays claim.

If human life is an oath, then suicide for me was like an oath recited backwards, a protest against the physical body that gave entrance to that first strange and violent ghost and all that followed. I would use my body as a vehicle for annihilation, and I kept those plans secret, teeth clenched, mouth like the silencer on a gun.

Tuesday.

Dearest,

I feel certain that I am going mad again: I feel we can't go through another of those terrible times. And I shan't recover this time. I begin to hear voices, & can't concentrate. So I am doing what seems the best thing to do. You have given me the greatest possible happiness. You have been in every way all that anyone could be. I don't think two people could have been happier till this terrible disease came. I can't fight it any longer, I know that I am spoiling your life, that without me you could work. And you will I know. You see I can't even write this properly. I can't read. What I want to say is that I owe all the happiness of my life to you. You have been entirely patient with me & incredibly good. I want to say that — everybody knows it. If anybody could

12

To Leonard Woolf
Tuesday (18 March 1941)

Dearest,

I feel certain I am going mad again. I feel we can't go through another of those terrible times. And I shan't recover this time. I begin to hear **voices**, and I can't concentrate. So I am doing what seems the best thing to do. **You have given me** the greatest possible happiness. You have been in every way all that anyone could be. I don't think two people could have been happier till **this terrible disease** came. I can't fight any longer. I know that I am spoiling your life, that without me you could work. And you will I know. You see I can't even write this properly. I can't read. What I want to say is I owe all the happiness of my life to you. You have been entirely patient with me and incredibly good. I want to say that - **everybody knows it**. If anybody could have saved me it would have been you. **Everything has gone** from me but the certainty of your goodness. I can't go on **spoiling** your life any longer.

I don't think two people could have been happier than we have been.

V.

The time it almost worked, I stood before the bathroom mirror in my parents' home, cupping water in the palm of my right hand to swallow the pills in my left. There were three-hundred-and-twelve pills in all. My mouth was as dry as a bone wind, and the capsules kept sticking to my tongue. I expected to feel something powerful—relief perhaps, fear, or even regret, but there was only the urgency of the poltergeist inside. From somewhere far away, my old self was speaking. "You are killing yourself," she warned. "You are killing yourself."

I hid all the vials in the back of a bathroom drawer and lay down on the living room sofa. My parents continued to watch television. My sister continued to ignore me from behind her closed bedroom door. I wrote a brief letter, which my mother would later remark was of poor quality for a writer, and then they switched off the lights, locked the doors, and everyone went to sleep.

The act of taking my own life is not something **I am** doing without **a** lot of thought. I don't believe that people should take their own lives without deep and thoughtful **reflection** over a considerable period of time. I do believe strongly, however, that the right to do so is one of the most fundamental rights that anyone in a free society should have. For me much **of the world** makes no sense, but my feelings about what I am doing ring loud and **clear** to an inner ear **and** a place where there is no self, only **calm**.

Love always, Wendy

I coded that night. Coded again. Died and was resurrected, but only because my mother saved me. I spent three weeks on life support, woke up, and walked around for an entire week I have no memory of—an amnesiac event is what they call it. The first thing I remember is standing in the bleak light of an inpatient mental facility wearing bloody pajama pants. There's a payphone in my hand.

Get me out of here, I'm saying, but to whom?

They gave me lithium three times a day, the pale yellow orb of it. On my tongue, the sacrament of it. All my eyelashes fell out. I told myself they were an offering. That they were black boughs placed upon the graves of everything that ever haunted me.

It was two years before I could focus long enough to read and write again.

"The past," writes Claudia Rankine, "is a life sentence, a blunt instrument aimed at tomorrow."

But only if you let it, I told myself. *Only if you let it.*

To BoddAH *pronounced*

Speaking from the tongue of an experienced simpleton who obviously would rather be an emasculated, infantile complainee. This note should be pretty easy to understand. All the warnings from the punk rock 101 courses over the years. Since my first introduction to the, shall we say, ethics involved with independence and the embracement of your community has proven to be very true. I haven't felt the excitement of listening to as well as creating music along with reading and writing for too many years now. I feel guilty beyond words about these things. For example when we're back stage and the lights go out and the manic roar of the crowd begins it doesn't affect me the way in which it did for Freddie Mercury who seemed to love, relish in the love and adoration from the crowd. which is something I totally admire and envy. The fact is, I can't fool you. Any one of you. It simply isn't fair to you or me. The worst crime I can think of would be to rip people off by faking it and pretending as if im having 100% fun. Sometimes I feel as if I should have a punch in time clock before I walk out on stage. I've tried everything within my power to to appreciate it (and I do, God, believe me I do, but it's not enough). I appreciate the fact that I and we have affected and entertained a lot of people. I must be one of those narcissists who only appreciate things when they're gone. I'm too sensitive. I need to be slightly numb in order to regain the enthusiasm I once had as a child. On our last 3 tours I've had a much better appreciation for all the people I've known personally and as fans of our music, but I still can't get over the frustration, the guilt and empathy I have for everyone. There's good in all of us and I think I simply love people too much. So much that it makes me feel too fuckings sad. The sad little, sensitive, unappreciative, pisces, Jesus man! Why don't you just enjoy it? I don't know! I have a goddess of a wife who sweats ambition and empathy and a daughter who reminds me too much of what I used to be. Full of love and joy, kissing every person she meets because everyone is good and will do her no harm. And that terrifies me to the point to where I can barely function. I can't stand the thought of Frances becoming the miserable self destructive, death rocker that I've become. I have it good, very good, and I'm grateful, but since the age of seven I've become hateful towards all humans in general. Only because it seems so easy for people to get along and have empathy. Empathy! Only because I love and feel sorry for people too much I guess. Thank you all from the pit of my burning nauseous stomach for your letters and concern during the past years. I'm too much of an erratic, moody, baby! I don't have the passion anymore and so remember, its better to burn out than to fade away. peace love, Empathy. Kurt Cobain

Frances and Courtney, I'll be at your altar.

please keep going Courtney,

for Frances

for her life which will be so much happier

without me. I LOVE YOU I LOVE YOU!

Thank you all **from the pit of my burning,** nauseous stomach for your letters and concern during the past years. I'm too much of an erratic, moody baby! **I** don't have the passion anymore, and so **remember**, **it's better to burn** out than to fade away.

Peace, love, empathy.
Kurt Cobain

Frances and Courtney, I'll be **at your alter**.
Please keep going Courtney, for Frances.
For her life, which will be so much happier without me.

I **LOVE** YOU, I LOVE YOU!

I've said that suicide is caused by a poltergeist that lives inside. But that is truer of my life before lithium. Suicide comes to me now as something external—as, from Homer's *Odyssey*, a Siren song—and each day, I do my best to battle the Sirens as Odysseus did, ears plugged with beeswax, body strapped to the mast. For I know the Sirens, oh the Sirens, they sing so slow and sweet.

It has been said of the Sirens that if we could only find a way to sail past their sweet music, they would fall lifeless into the sea. Having succumbed and been saved several times, I know better. Beneath the Golden Gate Bridge, where the bay shines bean-green over blue, a Siren will always lay in wait for me. It's been so long since I heard one singing, but I am no less afraid. In *The Silence of the Sirens*, Kafka writes:

> Now the Sirens have a still more fatal weapon than their song, namely their silence. And though admittedly such a thing never happened, it is still conceivable that someone might possibly have escaped from their singing; but from their silence certainly never.

No More Games. No More Bombs. No More Walking. No More Fun. **No More** Swimming. 67. That **is** 17 years past 50. 17 more than I **needed** or wanted. Boring. I am always bitchy. No Fun — for anybody. 67. **You are getting Greedy**. Act your **old** age. Relax — This won't **hurt**.

—Hunter S. Thompson

To re-enter the world of the living, to redirect neural pathways, or even make a plan that extends beyond dying next Tuesday, this, ironically, has become my life's work. For the better part of a decade, suicide was my only plan. And though I cannot say this with certainty, I believe I have moved beyond that now.

The question, of course, is how. How did I move beyond it? And the answer, I fear, is so intricate, so deeply nuanced, that I can never know it for certain.

What I do know: I wanted to write a book. And I convinced myself I couldn't die until that book was published. For three years, that plan was enough to keep me alive, though just barely. And then one day there was love, a love that had nothing to do with me, a love based solely upon the beauty I saw in someone else. Slowly, searchingly, I became accountable to that person, to that love. Wound by wound, I was healing because it is as Rumi says: The wound is the place where the light enters you.

To be clear, no one can kill or save a suicidal person. But for those to whom the Sirens call and call, it is crucial to take what you can get when you can get it. Even the tiniest things can sustain you, keep you alive for one more moment, and those moments will come to something—days, weeks, even years. And one day you'll allow for the possibility that no matter how good your reason is for wanting to die, there might be another way out.

***

There was this moment after my nearly successful suicide attempt when I looked from my hospital window to the rushed and ragged streets below and saw, beyond the squalor, a fierce, utopian beauty that reminded me of Campanella's *City Of the Sun*. As I watched people board buses, cop drugs, and stamp out cigarettes, this singular sentence rose to the surface: *please, just give me one more chance to be* in it.

It was only a sentence. It was only a moment—I went back immediately to wishing I was dead, but now I had a tool, I had something to work with, and that thing, however fleeting, was possibility.

No matter who you are or what you've done, there is beauty inside of you. Perhaps it is only a sliver, but within that sliver, your energy, creativity, kindness, and resilience are stored. You are free to go on hating the other parts of yourself. It is as you wish. But I am here to tell you that no matter what happens, no matter how muted or inaccessible that beauty feels, you have to hold onto it, and believe in it with the fervor of someone who is born again. If you can do that, even for one moment each day, that beauty will begin to sustain you. You will grow into it, and in doing so become more whole than you ever imagined.

Because the truth is, recovery, like suicide, starts with something small.

And someday the darkness that nearly defeated you will serve as a counterpoint, a mode of gratitude, for all the light you've built inside of you.

"Treachery is beautiful," wrote Jean Genet, "if it makes us sing."

This is a call to the damaged, the suicidal, and the mentally ill who feel as though they are drowning in darkness. I see you. I see your beauty. Hold fast to it. You are convinced, at this point, that you are all alone. I thought that too. But somewhere in the night, in every city, in every country, all around the world, there is a choir filled with people like you and me, and somehow, against all odds, we are singing.

ASKING FOR IT

When I was a girl, the thing I loved most was the game "Light as a Feather." Back then, I felt weightless when any girl had her hands on me, so lying there with six girls' fingers tucked beneath my body, I'd float to the ceiling, flushed and breathless. The touching was permissioned, so I could just enjoy it, though there was of course that fear of the occult. In the days that followed the game, I'd worry about the evil spirits that might've entered me. I'd lie awake feeling something of the devil a-flicker inside.

"Light As A Feather" was a ritual performed in murmuring secrecy. It was sexy and witchy, but did not require me to invite anyone or anything inside. "Ouija," on the other hand, was a kind of penetration I was not yet prepared for, a game my mother called *the occult version of asking for it.*

* * *

There are many reasons why in girlhood, we become necessarily preoccupied with possession. It makes sense—the fascination, as you are trying so desperately to grow into your body, with the dark thing that would drag you away. For girls are taught that the zenith of our lives occurs when we are most deeply inhabited by another. It is no coincidence, in *The Exorcist*, that the devil selects Regan for writhing. She is preteen, which means most poised to be entered.

* * *

Once upon a time, everything carnal or feral in me was made, by faith, moribund. For fourteen years, my body remained this way—untouchable, untouched.

Once upon a time, I had no idea what I felt like inside. I'd lie in bed at night, fingers pinned beneath the small of my back so that god would not mistake a single movement for a sin.

It was only a matter of time before I was broken open.

* * *

He was, at the time, my best friend. When I wouldn't let him kiss me, he shoved his fingers in my mouth. They were cold and smelled sharply of clementines.

And then it happened that he wormed my clothes away, and made me try things on, made me spin in a circle, motioning with his finger, a three-hundred-and-sixty-degree humiliation.

He choked me out on the heart-shaped canopy bed my father built for me when I was a little girl. There was a maglite under the mattress I used to read past my bedtime, and he fished it out and beat me with it until I agreed to lie still.

"I love you," he said, like I was an idiot not to know it. "I love you."

As he entered me, the room went black and filled with tiny stars. I had no idea I was so connected inside.

It was over for maybe minutes, and then it was never over.[1]

* * *

For months afterward, I avoided the eyes of my mother, father, and sister. I was worried they could tell by my face that I was changed. And then there was the feeling that everyone could see and smell my hymen ripped open, that the bruised triangle between my legs would point now only to what was missing.

I kept thinking, this creature, this monster, that my friend whom I loved turned out to be—was it there all along? Or was it culled from his body by my body, twirling as his finger guided me, tracing slow circles in the air?

* * *

In the game "Bloody Mary," where girls summon a murderous spirit in the mirror, the point is not to invite evil, to stir

---

1 Heather McHugh

the supernatural pot. To summon evil is to acknowledge its inevitability, to address that each moment spent in safety feels a lot like holding your breath. If being a girl means leaving this world in little pieces, let's get it over with. In chanting, let us exact some small control; let it be clear when and how we are asking for it.

* * *

Sleep was something to be avoided then. Within sleep, all the hidden things choiring like starlings.

The dream in which the graveyard slides into the sea, and I drink the water clogged by corpses' long, still-growing hair.

The dream where I feel safe from harm in a field of sunflowers until one by one, they give me up like a name they swore they'd take to the grave.

So much of my life was spent in that blue hour of morning, too early for waking and too late to fall asleep. I'd put myself in a kind of trance watching bloody true crime television. Like melancholic music when your heart is broken, sometimes the only thing you can do with a feeling is lean into it.

Fictional shows in which rapists were captured and punished enraged me. I preferred survivors of torture talking straight to the camera. Stalked, abducted, raped, shot at point-blank range. Then burned, tossed in a trunk, tied with rebar to a desert stone. The actresses reenacting the story crawling so convincingly across lush lawns in blood-soaked nightgowns or running through a dark wood with only half of their heads attached.

A documentary about Seattle singer Mia Zapata, who wrote a song about being murdered and spread in pieces all over town just before being killed by a stranger who strangled her with her own sweatshirt.

A documentary about the Tate murders, in which the crime scene photo of Abigail Folgers shows her less heiress, more lawn stain. Her last words to the man stabbing her: "You've got me. I'm already dead."

Maybe I was morbid to find comfort or, at the very least, distraction in these stories which were gruesome beyond my imagination. But I needed a break from the narrative I was living. The one where girls in my town were fish that fill a manmade lake, or fair chase pheasants set loose in the forest. The narrative where being hunted was the only thing they ever had in mind for us.

On a popular daytime talk show, footage of a body being exhumed. There are machines to help with the unearthing of the burial vault and tools to break its seal, revealing a cherry-colored casket still draped in withered white roses. The shock of these bright colors coming out of the dirt makes it seem as though the casket too could be pried open to reveal a girl who is more like a Russian doll than a decomposing body or even a girl who would open her eyes, like the murder never happened, and say: *I feel like a wet seed wild in the hot blind earth.*[2]

* * *

When as children, my sister and I named Ken dolls after our enemies and buried them alive beneath the evergreens, and when we dug up dead frogs from the glittery coffins we made for them, praying over their tiny souls in tongues of necromancy, these were not merely games to us, though that is what we said. We knew survival would depend increasingly upon our relationship to resurrection.

* * *

And so, just as the corn was silking, all I could think about was driving till I hit the Pacific, becoming for all intents and purposes a ghost.

You see, I come from a town where no one leaves and there's only one way a girl goes missing. Every few years, weighted to the bottom of a golf course pond or stuffed in a storm drain she will be discovered, made Legend.

You see I come from a town where there's only one way a girl is made Legend.

And in that town, that the air does not ring with them, that the new crocuses do not chatter with what has become of

2 William Faulkner

them, that the hushed ground is filled with them where they will remain forever, it is that more than anything that gave me the courage to leave.

Give me a world, I said aloud to no one. *You have taken the world I was.*[3] And a new world opened for me, by and by.

Each night in that blue light, they flickered across the ceiling. Pretty girls turned hungry ghosts who wanted to leave with me. I could see each of their lives like little boats upon the water, bright first, then burning, then snuffed out by the breakers of the sea.

I will not say to you that the Legends as I experienced them were real, that I can prove how the room filled with strange heat, buoyed by their breath.

What I'm saying is whether they were real or mere projections of the mind seen with intense clarity, we belonged to one another. And knowing them, what was done to them, gave me one hundred new reasons to survive.

* * *

I began at dawn through the green maze of corn, an achingly familiar crop that dizzied suddenly with its vastness, its flickering infinity. I drove all day long, straight through Des Moines' end-of-the-world darkness, where I made believe the few flickering lights were lanterns of the last survivors. Throughout Nebraska, day and night, earth and sky fused together, falling like a white sheet over me. That such

---

3 Anne Carson

monotony gave way to mountains was its own little miracle, though I couldn't decide at first whether they made me feel sheltered or loomed over. By the time I got to Oregon, the clouds seemed close enough that you could reach your hand through the sunroof and come back with a fistful of nimbostratus. And when at last I reached Seattle, lush and so fervently green it bordered upon narcotic, I knew for certain I would find heaven there.

* * *

The first thing I did was drive to the corner of 24th Avenue and South Washington Street, the place where Mia Zapata was made Legend. It felt like the only right place to start. Twenty years had passed since her death, something like five-thousand-five-hundred-and-twenty days of rain, and it seemed to me she still smudged the earth, though there was nothing of her spirit there, which I knew would move through darkened rooms bright as aurora borealis.

It was like stepping inside a house where you intuit immediately that something horrible has happened, except that there were no walls around it, making it that much harder to escape.

* * *

Aside from my books, I didn't want anything that home had threaded through. Everything else I burned, or left on the side of the road. What I needed, more than anything, was a perfect loneliness, pure and cold and bright. I found a studio two streets east of where Mia had lived when she'd been alive. With the apartment empty but for a mattress, windows clean, ceilings high, walls freshly white, I loved Seattle, which was more a city in the evening when its greenery folded into darkness. That first night, there was whiskey, and the Legends partnered and danced sweetly across the ceiling, and Nina Simone sang to a lover I hadn't met yet: *You're spring to me/all things to me/don't you know you're life itself?*

* * *

Back in high school, there were girls I loved for their beauty, and for their ability to receive pleasure without needing to return it. I would learn little things about them—a favorite song, a moon sign, so I could joke that we were star-crossed or destined depending—but I did not use or remember their names. I wanted them for the way they kissed, the way they moved and sounded in the dark, that they smelled of rosehip and jasmine or Parliaments and Jameson, that beneath my tongue, they'd rise to the ceiling like steam. The only girls I named were the girls with whom things went terribly wrong.

For instance, there was I Should've Loved A Thunderbird Instead[4], who threw a brick through the window of my car, filled the driver's seat with mayonnaise, and lit all of my shoes on fire before trying to fuck me in the driveway of my parents' home.

---

4 Sylvia Plath

There was What Spring Does To The Cherry Trees[5], who had feverish dreams I was the devil and tried, on more than one occasion, to spoon holy water into my hair before accosting me one day when I was at the dentist, marching right up to the chair to hit me in the face with the zippered end of her leather jacket.

In both instances, the authorities had to be called, and I authored wild explanations that absolved me entirely. I did not learn, in either instance, that for all the charm in the world, I would always be out of my depth until I could become a woman who could set her heart on something.

* * *

My favorite book as a girl was Truman Capote's *In Cold Blood*. I found myself in the farewell letter Willie-Jay addresses to Perry, one the novel's killers:

> You are a man of extreme passion, a hungry man not quite sure where his appetite lies, a deeply frustrated man striving to project his individuality against a backdrop of rigid conformity. You exist in a half-world suspended between two superstructures, one self-expression and the other self-destruction.

The juxtaposition of individuality and conformity could be true of anyone, as could the notion of existing in a half-world. What frightened me then was the misplaced hunger, the way

5 Pablo Neruda

33

that Perry, pulled by confusion and desire, became a killer, a grown man who had yet to understand his appetite.

The trouble with being a girl is that you are expected to trade craving for hunger, hunger the specter that looms over you even as you sleep. And this makes you feel like a predator, a prowler in the lambs' midst.

Being both evangelical and gay from birth, I worried at purity balls that my sinner's skin would singe my satin gown. I was made to wear a purity ring that only a wedding ring could remove—this, an offering of love from my earthly and heavenly fathers.

What I knew that they did not: If god made me, he made me an aberration of nature. Try as I might to people the wedding chapels of my imagination, there were other things consuming me, other fires, which burned the bridegrooms and leveled the altars to ash.

It was with this same burning that I left my hometown, determined to find what I wanted and, for the first time in my life, to ask for it.

* * *

I learned Seattle by watching it like a television. Learned, for example, that I would need to trade my thick Midwestern skin for indifference. Learned that a morning's bleariness was known to burn away like a marine layer, at which point the branches, hanging lush and wet and low, flickered for a bit in the wide pinking light. And on those days, people would stand in the street with reverence, or perhaps I imagined it that way. In any case, it made me feel that I was less alone.

* * *

I met her at a bar called Flowers, quiet and dark, three whiskies in.

From the start it was almost too much to look at her, so I stared instead out the windows, balmy with breath, tracing my fingers through their slow sweat.

When I worked up the nerve to be near her I was hooked right away by the friction between the few cautious words she afforded me and the way she knew, like no one had ever known, how to own me with her hot, hungry look. Those eyes that reduced continents to kindling, crisping planets of the Milky Way until the known universe scattered like ash from a cigarette's sleeve and in that bar, it was only the two of us. And in that moment, I was the first woman ever made or the last one alive at the end of the world.

 We compared scrapes born of war stories, and secretly, I named hers after summer constellations.

Southern Crown.

Northern Crown.

Arrow.

Archer.

Shield.

When I touched myself and was close to coming, I whispered her name, evoking her: a séance.

In the nights that followed, she was the specter. Bright, inscrutable orb darting the darkened room.

* * *

Every day the Legends got hungrier. I could hear the grinding of each twinkling maw. We were all starving in our own way, them because they'd been denied their rightful lives as women, me as a woman with the world before her too frightened and scarred to do a damn thing about it.

My days with them were lucid dreams.

Their stories swirled around me, and if I wanted, I could pluck one from the air and ask her.

Legend whose body was discovered in the dumpster behind Dot Liquor.

Legend who was murdered while playing Bloody Mary in the mirror.

Legends whose sweet mouths appeared still singing in the water, multiples of Millais's Ophelia.

Legend three days shy of her sweet sixteen birthday party, who received instead the party where everyone searches and searches, finding nothing in the end but a crawl space filled with bone.

* * *

I say that I asked them for their stories, but over time, the room became cacophonous. It was sometimes hard to remember I wasn't one of them. I was beginning to feel like my body was an "Ouija" board full of vague answers: *yes, no, goodbye.* Forever anticipating that moment where the wind shifts and the room moves from carefree to electric and malevolent.

The ghost I knew by heart was Mia. She was the only one who moved through the world with me. It was, after all, her neighborhood, and she was nice enough to show me around. We spoke through a kind of telekinesis, girl to ghost, and although it is strange to say so, Mia was my first Seattle friend. I would learn I wasn't the only one who felt that way, that many girls in Seattle were descendants of Mia, beautiful and strange but because of her story, less innocent, walking home from the Comet Tavern, their keys tiny knives between their fingers, their eyes two fierce dogs gone hunting in the night.

* * *

In Buddhism, there is a creature known as the Hungry Ghost, a spirit characterized by great craving and eternal starvation. Small of mouth, narrow of throat, Hungry Ghosts are all desire, with no way to satiate. Sometimes they'll receive a drop of water which evaporates upon the lips, or food, which bursts into flames before they can swallow. Every iota of desire comes with the consequence of pain, and being a woman had me like a Hungry Ghost. I am no longer willing to forfeit the wild and beautiful things I thirst for all for some craving gone quiet.

What I want now is a balance between woman and ghost.

A courage that has nothing to do with survival.

I want to eat a Clementine without thinking of his cold fingers.

I want Mia to eat my heart from cupped hands as Beatrice did Dante's, and for everyone to vow on her behalf: I will not let him make of me a craven thing when bravery is so much sweeter.

I want to never forget the Legends, but to set them free, or to trap them in a lucid dream from which I will myself awake, so that I may finally see past them, see instead the first sailboats of morning upon the water, salty and cerulean, and wonder how I got so lucky. And wonder I am alive to know it at all.

"I want to be with someone who knows secret things," Rilke said, "or else alone." And I would like that to be my love letter to her.

I want her to see in perfect detail the things that might have destroyed me, and how I chose beauty instead. I want her to know so she never doubts it again that she is commensurate of that beauty.

I want to move into the terror and the awe of this rare and beautiful thing between us, and hold there until we forget who we are, or how we might ruin one another, for as close and as long as she'll let me.

And if ever she asks, without a word, I will gently let her go.

HOLY SACRAMENT

When I was a child, my father was a purveyor of meat. Our refrigerator was frequently packed with raw muscle and glinting bone. Opening the refrigerator door overwhelmed the senses with the pungent stench of decomposition, death, spoils of the hunt. My milk and grapes mingled nervously in the graveyard of our icebox, growing sticky from the fluids gushing down.

A neighborhood boy told me red meat and cigarettes are bad for your flavor, that you must eat fresh fruit to sweeten the taste of your cum. And it was at this point it first occurred to me that I existed, perhaps, in order to be devoured.

* * *

Each of us begins as an embryo and then, a myth is set in motion.

What gender we will be assigned.

Whose moods and features we might inherit.

What mirror we will hold to the people who parent us.

You don't have to look at an ultrasound photograph long to realize its Rorschach quality.

I was weeks old when a minister performed the rite of holy baptism—a crime scene traced in oil across my forehead—while Father kept my squirming body still. Communion, the act of taking the body of christ into my mouth, was a privilege I would earn through the demonstration of knowledge. But then, they taught me in Sunday school that I was wicked for wanting knowledge, that I would bleed every month as payment for a single act of curiosity committed at the dawn of time.

From the moment it first appeared, I hated my period. I felt it reduced my body to the recitation of an ancient sin. I locked myself in the bathroom and screamed from the tub in a six-hour standoff. When I learned that starvation was an effective way to curb menstruation, I began throwing food in the trash, or over the deck railing, sometimes balling it up and submerging it in a tall glass of skim milk.

It took me years to realize that by forsaking paradise, Eve engendered a world where we split atoms, write symphonies, and move with ease through the Milky Way. That if knowledge is the reason women bleed, we should consider that blood holy sacrament.

* * *

The way evangelical Christianity works is that women are the sacrament. A girl's parents issue her a purity ring, which shall be worn until replaced by a wedding band. Her male peers, subject to the same doctrine, will not be required to accessorize, nor will they be expected to attend purity balls—formal events where female children dressed in taffeta and lace swear to God and congregation that Dad's in charge of their body until an approved husband takes the reins. These ceremonies are conducted before girls understand what sex is, and the central message is this: Your body is not your own.

* * *

But what is a girl to do when all attempts at chastity are rendered meaningless?

What was I to do when I was raped at fourteen?

And again at nineteen?

And again at twenty-seven?

In the story of my body, the hardest thing to figure is this: jesus, nailed willingly to a cross, dead, then resurrected three days later, is known for performing the ultimate sacrifice. But when I was dragged by my hair down a deserted beach, bitten, beaten, and derided, no one saw this as sacrifice, nor did god laud me from his heaven.

I know this because in childhood, I often turned to the Bible, which clearly states that a rape victim is to be stoned alongside her rapist, or else purchased from her father for fifty pieces of silver and forced to marry said rapist for the remainder of her natural life.

If you wish to live in this world as a true Christian, you are required to hold a single belief: that jesus died so brutal men could be forgiven.

Meanwhile, if you're a woman who walks the earth with two cheeks bruised from turning, and you wonder why forgiveness, why mercy, is never extended to you, it is best to quiet your confusion with scripture.

1 Corinthians 6:20—

You are not your own, for you were bought with a price. So glorify God in your body.

* * *

Mother, a gifted seamstress, made me a mermaid the Halloween of my eighth year. There was a flesh-colored body suit with a soft purple seashell bra and a scaly emerald tale that glittered in sunlight. We spray-painted my hair bright red and applied red lipstick so I would look just like Disney's Ariel.

Though I made for a very conservative mermaid, I felt a shift immediately in the way men looked at me. It was as though, for the first time, they had been granted permission. In the narrow light of their eyes, there was hunger. And amusement. And in their speech, the desire to make their every impulse known. I was not a sexually aware eight-year-old, if such a child can be said to exist. I was awkward, misshapen, and had yet to experience a single lick of lust. And there had been no indication from my father, who to this day has never said the word "sex" in front of me, that this was the kind of behavior I could expect from men. Being the center of so much attention was horrible, and I squirmed beneath it, though some small part of me was already confusing being stared at with being seen.

It was true that I had the body of a woman, breasts bigger than any of my teachers. Father wasn't capable of noticing such a thing, but Mother knew exactly what this meant.

After that Halloween, my level of social restriction was upgraded to serious. No leaving the yard. No babysitters with boyfriends or sleepovers with girls who had brothers. Looking back, I can't imagine how it must've felt to Mother, her eight-year-old daughter already a hunted thing, a reality of womanhood with which she was all too familiar.

* * *

Father approached the problem of my body conservatively. We walked the marsh and he used nature to illustrate god's plan for me.

"You see the male ducks?" he asked. "Do you notice their feathers are flashy? As opposed to the female ducks, whose feathers camouflage? Well, it's the male duck's job to attract attention, and the female duck's job to stay at home, where she'll be safe.

"You need to be more like the female duck," he said.

"Yes, dad," I answered.

I never asked if he saw any flaws in a plan that made males bright and seafaring and females doomed to a life crouching low among the cattails. I never told him that for women, life is more like the everglades, where pythons pulse and gators feed, and the bodies of missing girls bob beneath the river grass.

The disrespect I received from strangers, while alarming, was tame compared to the behavior of men who knew me.

A neighborhood friend mentioning casually that he wanted to fuck my sister and me at the same time.

An uncle spilling wine down my dress at a Christmas party in order to burst through my bedroom door while I was changing.

An accountant who slipped his hand between my legs whispering: "Beautiful girl, so, so beautiful."

Even if Father had known about all of these incidents, what could he have done? How could he have protected me? We are not talking, after all, about a series of strange occurrences. We are talking about an attitude, an onslaught, an atmosphere.

Here is something I know that Father does not: On their first date at an upscale restaurant, Mother got up to use the restroom, rounded the corner, and ran into a busboy who stuck two fingers inside of her. I know this because women speak easily with one another about all kinds of assault in the safety of one another's company. It is as common as breathing. Father doesn't know because Mother didn't want to ruin things—not their first date, and not the memory of it. Looked at in a certain light, my parents' love story, which made the formation of our family possible, began with a violation. A violation and a decision one person made to be silent so as not to shake the other from his kind but insular reality.

* * *

The same year Mother made me a mermaid, I received a marble rolling pin for Christmas. For baking, Mother said. It was so heavy I could barely lift it from its carved wooden cradle. I kept it under my pillow next to a box cutter I'd robbed from the garage and secreted away. I was armed always, and still before sleep each night the horrible feeling of my heart in my throat.

I placed a baby monitor beneath my sister's bed so I would know if anyone came for her in the night. I ran practice drills to ensure that from any room in the house, my parents could hear me screaming. I'd say my prayers (*and if I die before I wake*) then remain awake for hours, promising protection to my dolls through the obsessive recitation of Psalms.

At school, I was constantly called into the guidance counselor's office because I could write only of bodily harm. My victims, hunted down by psychopaths, were bludgeoned and brutalized.

The guidance counselor was convinced I was being abused at home, which made Mother furious.

"I don't know where she's getting this from," Mother insisted. "She's not even allowed to watch TV."

Sometimes, Mother would look at me as though weighing whether there was something evil inside.

"You're such a ghoul," she'd say to me. "Must you always be such a ghoul?"

I was not a ghoul. Being a ghoul, I imagined, would be accompanied by some sense of delight.

I was not abused, nor did I rely upon television for my daily dose of violence.

The fault was not my mother's as I suspect, and this is really saying something, that I was the most sheltered kid in town.

The truth is, my ghoulish nature was born of this and only this: I was an eight-year-old girl who woke up one morning in a woman's body.

I had eight years on this planet to prepare for the objectification and resulting violence anyone could see was imminent.

For me the question is singular. It is simple. It is this— was it my early exposure to rape culture, or the necessity of self-preservation that rose up out of it, that meant before anyone laid a hand on me, my innocence was already gone?

THE RETURN OF HUNGER

I can only say in the dark
how one Spring
I crushed a monarch midflight
just to know how it felt
to have something change
in my hands.

  —Ocean Vuong

Disordered eating was as much a part of my upbringing as arithmetic or prayer.

Each bland dinner began with the blood and the body of christ.

Every night my mother served us the same meal—steamed chicken and vegetables, which were carefully weighed on a small white scale in order to track portion size and caloric intake with precision.

Upon the kitchen counter was a cookie jar in the shape of a cow that mooed when you opened the lid. Only very rarely did it contain cookies.

It was meant to be a lesson.

It was meant to be a trap.

Memories of mealtime are so vivid that even in my adult life, it is difficult to separate present from past, as though eating could only exist inside the same shameful moment.

* * *

A girl is given a mantra, which is like a prayer:
A moment on the lips, a lifetime on the hips.
Nothing tastes as good as being thin feels.[4]

A girl is given a diet and, as the trends change, another and another:
Alkaline. Atkins. Baby Food. Blood Type. Cabbage Soup. Master Cleanse. Mediterranean. Paleolithic. Slimfast. South Beach. Weight Watchers. Zone.

A girl is given aid:
Adderall. Dexatrim. Hodroxycut. Metabolife.

A girl is given the opportunity to push herself:
The ipecac diet. The finger down your throat diet. The swallowing of saturated cotton balls diet. The laxative diet. The

---

4 Attributed to Kate Moss

cigarette diet. Even the Breatharian diet, in which nourishment is derived solely from sunlight and air.

If it is as Plath ventures, that "dying/ is an art," then disordered eating is the central artistic medium in which girls are instructed and supported. As women, we pass this curse from generation to generation, enforcing the very practices that made *us* ill and held *us* down.

For over a decade prior to her first pregnancy, my mother controlled her figure and her hunger by chewing sugar-free cinnamon gum and eating exactly seven saltine crackers a day. In sharp contrast, pregnancy must've felt to my mother like being violently possessed.

She tells stories about blacking out and coming to in the McDonald's parking lot, the flavor of burgers and apple pies on her tongue.

She had nightmares that we were born so small and starving we disappeared in the sheets.

When it was time to be born, my mother's hips proved too small, so my sister and me were ripped from her body like bad spirits in a séance gone wrong.

My mother did her best to make healthy choices while I was in utero, but I know plenty of women with mothers who refused to "eat for two," women whose first diet began in the womb, where they grew from a cradle of bone.

* * *

The great love of my childhood was my grandmother, the well meaning, rightwing matriarch who firmly believed that beauty was a woman's greatest power. She took me to the K-Mart superstore every Friday so I could select another doll to inhabit my Barbie universe. By age six, I had everything a little girl could dream of: dozens of Barbies, three corvettes and a safari jeep, a spa, an ice cream store, and a cul-de-sac of Dream Houses. An embarrassment of riches but for one thing: I fucking hated Barbie, along with that basic tween, Skipper, and the most likely closeted Ken.

Barbie's sexuality was confusing to me. Why the irremovable underpants? Why large breasts but no vagina? What did that say about vaginas? About breasts? And why, I wondered, did my friends make their Barbies and Kens scissor? Why did my babysitter enjoy making Ken talk dirty to me?

* * *

Germaine Greer: Whenever we treat women's bodies as aesthetic objects without function we deform them.

* * *

In their interactive, multi-media collaboration entitled *Doll Games*, artists Shelley and Pamela Jackson describe the eroticism of their dolls, claiming they knew the dolls' bodies better than their own. The Jacksons speak of their Barbies' private lives as "perfect."

"I identified with their hard dumb inexpressiveness," Shelley Jackson writes. "It was how I felt too: my real life did not show on the outside. The dolls clacked together, their bodies all beak, all shell. Despite this, everything about them was erotic."

The Jacksons say of their dolls, "their secrets were ours."

Was it for lack of imagination that I eyed my Barbies suspiciously, doing my best to match the stoicism hidden carefully beneath all their lipsticked, saccharine cheer?

* * *

In her doll-hating Opus, *The Bluest Eye*, Toni Morrison writes, "Adults, older girls, shops, magazines, newspapers, window signs—all the world agreed that a blue-eyed, yellow-haired, pink-skinned doll was what every girl child treasured."

When the novel's Claudia is gifted such a doll for Christmas, it is with this breathless incantation: "This is beautiful, and if you are on this day 'worthy,' you may have it."

"What was I supposed to do with it?" Claudia wonders. "Pretend to be its mother?"

Eventually, Claudia rips that blue-eyed, yellow-haired, pink-skinned doll to pieces. It is hard to imagine a reader who does not cheer her on.

* * *

No part of me believed the Barbies were beautiful. Each time I held them, it was an interrogation of their shallow superiority, their embodiment of the feminine mystique. I felt they had to answer for the damaging ideals their bodies engendered, considered them monsters who deserved to be maimed. It might be said that the hatred of something as feminine as Barbie is not in keeping with the spirit of feminism, but then, I reasoned, these Barbies were not women. They were weekly reminders of a certain plastic perfection my chubby, queer, nerdy self would never attain.

"Dolls work like possession: the little girl's daemon occupies the helpless vessel of the doll," writes Shelly Jackson, but for the life of me, I could never find a way in.

* * *

One afternoon, pushed to my breaking point by a lunchroom bully who chanted "Miss Piggy," every time I ate, my sister and I declared war on our whole Barbie universe. She designed an amazing Chinese Water Torture Chamber. I made bombs from thumbtacks, pop rocks, and tea lights and left them in the elevator of every Dream House. When at last we deemed their torture sufficient, we cut the dolls in pieces with pruning shears, dumped their parts in a fish tank at the end of my bed and, because we were benevolent dictators, spent the rest of the week composing elegies.

* * *

Simone Weil: We must not wish for the disappearance of our troubles but for the grace to transform them.

* * *

In his poem, "Playing With Dolls," David Trinidad describes how every weekend morning, he'd sneak downstairs to play with his sisters' Barbie dolls.

> I'd finger each glove and hat and
> necklace and high heel, then put them on the dolls.
> Then I'd invent elaborate stories. A "creative" boy,
> I could entertain myself for hours. I liked to play
> secretly like that, though I often got caught. All
> my father's tirades ("Boys don't play with Barbies!
> It isn't normal!") faded as I slipped Barbie's
> perfect figure into her stunning ice blue and
> sea green satin and tulle formal gown.

To no one's surprise, Trinidad's poem does not have a happy ending.

> You're a boy,
> David. Forget about Barbies. Stop playing with dolls.

What is the lesbian's relationship to Barbie?
She cannot possibly embrace Barbie as subversive in the way David Trinidad could.

She cannot locate her fantasy in a eunuch Ken anymore than in the sleek contours of a doll who is meant to instruct or erase rather than entice.

So many girls I've dated speak of leaving Barbie dolls in their boxes, unloved and untouched, their poor Mothers crying straight through Christmas morning. This is what it looks like to be queer in Barbie universe—boys like David Trinidad dressing their sisters' Barbies in secrecy, and girls whose symbolically loaded Barbies are forced upon them.

* * *

In my early twenties, I subsisted on a diet of apples, green and whiskeys, neat.

Though I denied it at the time, thinness was the most important thing to me.

I was seeing five different women then, all of them sexy and thin, and my anorectic mindset masqueraded as a mode of control. If I could live on three hundred calories, I reasoned, I'd remain beautiful enough to keep each of them in my bed.

My refrigerator was barren, my cupboards aching with emptiness.

"Keep going," the hot bartender told me. "You are almost perfect."

Then I met J., who hated thinness. Who railed against the diet industry, and eating disorders, and girls with skinny asses. She would not accept my anorexia. She force-fed me healthy foods, spinach and sesame tofu and, compared to the other girls, her love for me felt positively nourishing.

She wanted a curvy girl. Tits and ass. Hourglass body. Is what she said.

Yet upon her living room wall was a framed poster of pin-up Betty Page in a size-small leather bikini. What was sexy about her, I wondered, to someone like J.? Were I reduced to my skeleton, I would never be as thin as the pinup of her dreams.

The truth about anorexia is that even when the behavior is dormant, the mind lies in wait for any excuse to resume.

I took the poster as permission to continue starving myself.

When we moved in together, she hung Betty on our bedroom wall. For the next six years, two cities, and three apartments, Betty presided over us, judging us, I believed, as we fought, fucked, and slept.

* * *

Marya Hornbacher: We turn skeletons into goddesses and look to them as if they might teach us how not to need.

* * *

In his 1987 film, *Superstar: The Karen Carpenter Story*, Todd Haynes replaces performers with Barbie Dolls in order to re-enact the final seventeen years of Karen Carpenter's life before her death from anorexia-related causes in February of 1983.

To reflect Carpenter's bodily deterioration, Haynes slims the Karen doll gradually, with a knife. The result is an uncanny hollowing out that perfectly embodies Carpenter's decline.

"It hardly seems more absurd," a critic noted, "to embody Karen Carpenter as an increasingly emaciated Barbie doll ... than to have her played by a workaday actress in a paint-by-numbers biopic."

In addition to the film's creative use of dolls, Haynes communicates with the viewer via occasional title cards, which prove insightful. The first reads:

> The self-imposed regime of the anorexic reveals a complex internal apparatus of resistance and control. Her intensive need for self-discipline consumes and replaces all her other needs and desires. Anorexia thus can be seen as an addiction and abuse of self-control, a fascism over the body in which the sufferer plays the parts of both dictator and the emaciated victim who she so often resembles.

To those who would argue that anorexia is about emulating the slim figures of movie stars, or desperately attempting to become conventionally beautiful, Haynes offers an alternative theory:

> In a culture that continues to control women through the commoditization of their bodies, the anorexic body excludes itself, rejecting the doctrines of femininity, driven by a vision of complete mastery and control.

* * *

Richard Siken: The fear: that nothing survives. The greater fear: that something does.

* * *

There have been times in my life when I was subjected to serious violence. In the aftermath, it was as though my muscles never made memory to begin with. My body forgot how to be a body, refusing the usual body things. Fucking Dancing. Bathing.

Touching. And being touched.

After the violence, I was horrified by the time I'd wasted obsessing over my body's thinness, its sexiness. How badly I treated my body back when it was relatively unscathed.

Rather than grow thinner, more delicate, I ate endlessly in bed, gaining over thirty pounds in a few months' time.

My mother spoke a lot back then about how gaining weight, how aging, renders the female body invisible.

It was all I wanted. To blend into the ether and disappear.

Roxanne Gay:

> When you're fat, no one will pay attention to disordered eating or they will look the other way or they will look right through you. You get to hide in plain sight. I have hidden in plain sight, in one way or another, for most of my life. Willing myself to not do that anymore, willing myself to be seen, is difficult.

Often, what got me through the week was the idea of never being seen again.

I left my house exactly once a day, driving the long, curving road that led to Carkeek Park. Wandering beneath the watery sun, I scouted locations.

Here, I'd say to myself. Just beyond the tide pools, where no child would find me.

Here, just before the orchard, alongside the salmon run.

Every day, new coordinates for the same shallow grave.

Every day, a new plan for disappearing.

It was the lowest point of my life, but it didn't last forever.

* * *

Fanny Howe: "The evidence of a successful miracle is the return of hunger."

* * *

After the emergence of multiple studies that linked Barbie's impossibly unrealistic body to an unhealthy body image in young girls, Mattel, Inc. finally announced a campaign to manufacture Barbies that represent "real women."

Mattel, Inc. would have us believe that they've invested in diversity and body positivity, but is that true? Can an organization that has knowingly compromised the body image of young girls have anyone's interests at heart but the shareholders and executives? One look at the new, "real," Barbie (a size ten, tops) tells me she is every bit as revolutionary as the new and improved, man-bun sporting Ken.

The real solution for girls is one that would put Mattel, Inc. out of business.

Fuck Barbie.

Teach a girl to code.

Put books, instruments, and microscopes in Barbie's place.

* * *

I used to believe that there was catharsis in destroying Barbie dolls, that it was a healthy way to reject the patriarchy. I see now that through such catharsis, the blame is merely redirected at women— in this case, women who embody the Barbie-esque.

Why should any form of beauty be subject to destruction?

Naomi Wolf: A culture fixated on female thinness is not an obsession about female beauty, but an obsession about female obedience.

The greatest lie the devil ever told is that women are *by nature* aggressive, competitive, and "catty" with one another. It is a myth that shifts insidiously from generation to generation. Every time women choose to invest in this myth, the joke is one hundred percent on us.

We need to stop making ourselves so thin that we slip through the cracks of history.

We need to stop starving our spirits and intellects long enough to find a way out.

Queer women, while not immune to patriarchy or the male gaze, are slightly less entangled in it. We have more freedom to author and reject standards of beauty, and we're well versed in forming communities in which we depend on one another. Because of this good fortune, it seems, we have a greater responsibility to light the way.

As I continue to seek wisdom about my body and the bodies of others, this is what I know to be true:

Each time you set eyes upon a woman, look for the thing that is strong and beautiful.

If a woman criticizes your body, disarm her with the sweetest, truest compliment you can muster.

If you feel driven to criticize a woman's body, know that that thought was planted in you, break free of it, and feel love for her body instead.

Most of all, remain hungry.

"It is impossible to forgive whoever has done us harm," writes Simone Weil, "if that harm has lowered us. We have to think that it has not lowered us, but has revealed our true level."

The revolution begins, the true level is revealed, the moment women consent to forgive one another.

THE TWIST

You are an unstitched doll learning her parts as she
loses them.

—Aziza Barnes

Some things can only be understood through retrospective
redefinition.

That we were *there* when they discovered the bodies.

That half the town was there, and no one knew.

When the police responded to the scene that August in
1995, they pulled the girls from the culvert pipe, peeled
them apart, and removed their bodies from the park in a
hushed, expedient manner so as not to disturb attendees of
the annual Milford Memories Fair.

It didn't take long to identify the bodies as best friends
Jennifer Wicks and Cassandra Fiolek, who hadn't run away
after all.

* * *

The summer of '95 was a sad time for my sister and me, even before the trauma of August.

Our parents, who hovered over us, were strangely absent, and though we could not work out why, the fault, we assumed, was ours.

Hidden away from the humid night and whoever might lurk within it, we dragged a television into my sister's closet, feeding home movies into the VCR.

We watched the movies with great concentration, wondering if "Florida" might foreshadow our abandonment. If "Xmas '88" revealed something unlovable about our true nature. If "Girls, Halloween" or "Dad On the News" contained naked glimpses of the soul.[1]

* * *

The violent history of deceptively bucolic Central Park did not begin with the murders of Cassandra and Jennifer.

January 4th, 1992. Fifteen-year-old Cynthia Jones and her boyfriend are brutalized by a masked man. The man ties the boyfriend to a tree. Abducts Cynthia at knifepoint. The cops blame the boyfriend until May 27th of that year, when serial killer Leslie Allen Williams confesses to murdering Cynthia and three other teenage girls. At the time of his arrest, Williams has already been convicted of multiple violent

---

1 Anne Carson, "The Glass Essay"

62

felonies. His psychiatric evaluation describes a true misogynist and sociopath whose central motivation is sadism.

His killing spree becomes known as "The Michigan Murders."

Three years later, when the bodies of Cassandra and Jennifer are discovered, it is stranger for the citizens of Milford than if, at that very park, lightning struck twice.

* * *

If the citizens of Milford felt that the murder of Cynthia Jones prepared them for the double homicide of Cassandra and Jennifer, they were mistaken. The details of the case are so brutal that even now, I want to be careful how I talk about it.

At trial, prosecuting attorney Donna Pendergast was quoted as saying, "We tell our children there are no monsters. They don't come out at night, they don't hide in the dark, they don't torture and kill little girls. This case will prove beyond any doubt that we delude ourselves."

* * *

In his taped confession, Aaron S. Stinchcombe (21), told police that on the day of the murder, he and friend Russell Oeschger (28), were befriended by Cassandra and Jennifer in Central Park. The girls asked if the men would purchase alcohol to celebrate their upcoming thirteenth birthdays. The men agreed, and plans were made to return to Central Park at midnight. Oeschger, who was homeless and living in the park at the time, purchased three bottles of liquor. As the girls slipped out Cassandra's window and headed to the park, the men sat at a picnic table near the woods, waiting.

Given that the girls were twelve and tasting liquor for the first time, it didn't take a lot to get them drunk. They rose from the table, laughing and dancing, turning sloppy cartwheels in the cool grass.

"We were having a good time," Stinchcombe told police.

At a certain point, Oeschger told Stinchcombe he was going to have sex with the girls, to which Stinchcombe said, "Ok, whatever."

As no one was shocked to learn, the girls resisted. They fought Oeschger with everything they had, and he flew into a rage. Separating the girls, he forced Jennifer toward the bathrooms, while Stinchcombe led Cassandra into the woods.

Oeschger raped and murdered Jennifer, then made his way to the woods to assist Stinchcombe with Cassandra. Oeschger raped Cassandra, then both men beat her to death. As the men debated how best to dispose of the bodies, Cassandra rose up from the ground screaming.

This was the way they silenced her:

Both men took Cassandra's face in their hands and twisted her head from her neck, chanting slowly, in unison, "wind up toy, wind up toy."

Cassandra was then stabbed, and the men stacked the girls' bodies in the culvert pipe. The bloody knife was later found throwing distance from the park, along idyllic Main Street.

* * *

Although Oeschger and Stinchcombe provided police with nearly identical confessions, Stinchcombe's attorney argued there was insufficient evidence to prove his client's premeditation, or any direct role in Jennifer's death.

The preliminary hearing for Oeschger was postponed for the expressed purpose of conducting a psychiatric evaluation.

The taped confessions of both men were introduced in two separate trials to two equally sickened juries. The men were convicted of first-degree premeditated murder and felony murder charges and were sentenced to life in prison without parole.

As many people remarked, the name of the festival, Milford Memories, took on a sinister meaning after that.

* * *

I was twelve the year of the murders, the same age as Cassandra and Jennifer. I was learning how to cook, forge report card signatures, and make sure my nine-year-old sister made her way to school each morning. I did my best but the truth is, I was underequipped and overwhelmed. My sister slept in my bed every night, insisting I hold her hand so I'd know if the murderers tried to take her away. We stashed steak knives all over the house and stretched wire across the windows, but nothing could protect us from the newly discovered fact that none of us, not a one of us, is safe.

It was a year equal parts anxiety and ennui. A year of moonlessness, which blackened the lake so that in darkness, it was indistinguishable from the land.

* * *

In a statement to the press, police chief John Daly was quoted as saying, "the girls went out there looking for a party and they found the wrong kind of party." As though the curiosity of two children justified their decomposing in a damp and shallow grave. The excitement of alcohol and older men lured Cassandra and Jennifer to the park that night—that much seems irrefutable.

"She was in that stage where she wanted to experiment with stuff like alcohol," Cassandra's brother explained.

But that's not what the police chief meant, and everyone knew it.

The story the chief was telling was one as old as time, the one in which the blame for murdered girls rests squarely upon the shoulders of the girls themselves, whose only real sin is lacking the internalized dialectic of terror designed to keep young ladies in their place. With his cavalier demeanor, Daly was laying out a lesson for the girls of Milford, one that would be repeated for the rest of our lives. We were being blamed, preemptively, for any and every violence that befell us.

From the police chief to pastors and parents all throughout the county, the deaths of Cassandra and Jennifer were the smug punch line in a game of *that's what you get.* To this day, people say it.

Boys, booze, sneaking out at night—well, that's what you get.

If you confront them with the fact that nobody deserves what those girls got, they'll say, *of course, of course, nobody does,* but they will not be shaken from their rhetoric.

It makes people fearful to think the problem is with law enforcement or the legal system. They don't want to see murder as the consequence of vagrancy laws that went unenforced. They refuse to examine the disturbing ways we socialize young men and women.

It is literally easier for most people to blame vicious, premeditated murder on two twelve-year-old girls.

Their wanderlust. Their disobedience. Their stupidity.

* * *

It is worth mentioning here that Cassandra was wary of strangers. That she knew Aaron Stinchcombe because he'd helped paint her family's house.

"He was her friend for a while, before all this," Cassandra's brother said.

In his confession, Stinchcombe confirmed this assertion when he revealed to the police Cassandra's final words: *What are you doing? I trusted you.*

* * *

In the house where I grew up, the neighborhood beach was directly across the street. Despite the fact you could see the beach from the front porch, my sister and I were not allowed to go alone. I spent many summers, face pressed to the window, as my unaccompanied classmates ran down the hill, cannonballing into the water, splashing around and having the time of their lives. The older I became, the more embarrassed I was to travel the neighborhood with my mother in tow, though for fear of hurting her feelings, I kept that to myself.

I do not blame my parents for this, but their paranoia and fear seeped into me.

* * *

When blame was being passed in the murders of Cassandra and Jennifer, Cassandra's mother, Renee Lang, seemed to be hit from all sides.

An early theory in the case was that the girls were targeted because Lang was a police dispatcher.

The other issue was that Lang admitted to slipping out of the house to play pool on the night of the murders, leaving the girls unsupervised. Jennifer's mother, Deborah Wicks, came after Lang in a wrongful death suit, claiming that, had Lang acted responsibly, she would've caught the girls crawling out their window, and the murders would not have happened.

"The ones that did it were convicted in a court of law," said Lang in an interview with the *Oakland Press*. "This is about money. This is blood money. It's not going to bring anybody back."

* * *

The night Robert Oeschger learned his son was arrested for the rape and murder of two twelve-year old girls, he slept soundly for the first time. Admitting he lived in fear of his son, he described installing bars on the doors and stashing a loaded gun under the bed. In an interview with the *Flint Journal*, Robert Oeschger was quoted as saying "I was a prisoner in my own home. Until now."

As far as I'm aware, Robert Oeschger's parenting skills were never called into question.

* * *

The details on where Jennifer is buried have never been released. But it is a matter of public record that Cassandra was buried in Milford Memorial Cemetery, just over one mile from the park where she was murdered. Pictured on Cassandra's gravestone: her latest school picture, a winged horse, and this epitaph: *Whoever harms a child shall never gain the kingdom of heaven.*

* * *

Avery F. Gordon, quoting Horkheimer and Adorno: "In the wake of disaster, we should experience true unity with the dead, as 'we, like them, are the victims of the same condition and the same disappointed hope.'"

* * *

As reported in the *New York Times* on August 15, 1995:

> The suspects have revealed at least two motives in the slayings, the police said: The girls were killed when the men realized they were having sex with minors, and one of the men wanted to be sent back to prison.

How anyone could mistake twelve-year-old girls turning cartwheels in the park for women of age is a genuine mystery, especially when you consider that one of the men was a family friend. As for getting sent back to jail, there are many ways to do that which do not include the rape and murder of children. Obviously. Add to these alleged motives the one about embittered criminals targeting Cassandra because of her mother's role in the police force, and you have yourself a fairly complex agenda.

It is here that I'd like to offer up my own little theory. It seems strange to me that it was not more seriously considered.

The true motive for raping and murdering Cassandra and Jennifer was the desire to rape and murder Cassandra and Jennifer.

Case closed.

* * *

As intensely overprotected children, my sister and I worried what the murders of Cassandra and Jennifer might mean for us, what new restrictions might be put in place.

Certainly my parents were horrified, and did their best to protect us from the details of the case while still utilizing it as a cautionary tale. Yet if anything, they appeared to be loosening the reins a little.

It was because we were older, maybe. Or because we proved we were trustworthy.

"They're tired of us," my sister said. "They're exhausted from all that smothering."

I suspected it was because what they feared most had already happened, and they believed that all of us would now be subject to some sort of heavenly reprieve.

* * *

"In the case of Cassandra and Jennifer," wrote prosecuting attorney Donna Pendergast, "I always wonder how two ne'er-do-wells could escalate from petty crimes to such diabolical and monstrous acts of murder. As to all three cases, I wonder what the odds are that such a seemingly idyllic setting in such a serene and quiet community would be the scene of such horrific evil not once but on two separate occasions only a few years apart. I'm sure that these questions will haunt me for the rest of my life."

The more haunting question, to me, was why there were only three murders in three years, when elsewhere, little girls died every day.

Or why, in the cases of Leslie Allen Williams, Russel Oeschger, and Aaron Stinchcombe, the common denominator was a rap sheet that read like a horror movie?

The danger was not coincidental, nor was it central to Milford. It was in the men, who the law saw fit to release, on multiple occasions, back into society.

"The American dream," writes Toni Morrison, "is innocence and clean slates and the future."

So that is what we let ourselves believe.

We are surprised in Milford when evil lands on our doorstep, relieved when it is reduced to a cautionary tale, and unaffected as the ugliness loses its resonance and rescinds into the night.

I visited my parents in Michigan this year, explaining over Sunday breakfast that I wanted to visit Central Park. That I was writing about the murders of Cassandra and Jennifer, and also the girl who was murdered in '92, what was her name?

"Cynthia Jones?" my father said a little too quickly. "The creep who killed her, he was a really bad guy."

"Like, in general?" I asked, "or did you know him personally?"

My parents exchanged a loaded look.

"We promised we would never tell you," my father said, "but he was staying with a friend of mine in the house kitty corner to us.

"See?" he gestured, "that one, across the street, the house right next to the beach."

Suddenly, my entire childhood snapped into focus.

My parents hovered over us because Leslie Allen Williams was our neighbor.

They eased up after he was locked away.

* * *

Avery F. Gordon: "If you let it, the ghost can lead you toward what has been missing, which is sometimes everything."

* * *

It's been suggested more than once that I have a macabre obsession with murdered girls.

The obsession part is fair, I suppose.

The deaths of Jennifer and Casey happened at an age where my conscience and awareness were forming. A little bit of investigating revealed parts of the world where women were practically an endangered species.

The fact that Jennifer and Casey were twelve, like I was, made their murders more resonant somehow.

The horrible things that happened to those girls: it could've been, it should've been, me. To come face to face with a serial killer, all I had to do was cross the street.

What was it, I wondered, that separated me from Cynthia Jones, Jennifer Wicks, Cassandra Fiolek, or any murdered girl?

Obsessively, I tallied the reasons and arrived every time at dumb luck.

Given that I am alive and so many are dead, I'd have to be a monster to look away.

Admittedly, I don't know what to do with this yet. I know that it isn't helpful to loiter about in other people's tragedies. But it is my responsibility to bear witness, to look closely and unflinchingly at terrible things that I'm tempted to shy away from. I want to extend a hand into the moonless dark where countless girls were swallowed up and never seen again, and swear to them, every one of them, your sacrifice matters. And I will not allow you to be forgotten.

PHANTOM FARES

Japan, 2011. A magnitude nine undersea megathrust earthquake hits Tōhoku with such force it causes the earth's axis to shift by several inches. Along the coastline, fifty fires ignite at once. An oil refinery explodes into flame and thick black smoke billows from that burning. Moments later, a one-hundred-and-thirty-three foot tsunami rushes over the land, swallowing buildings and fishing vessels with terrifying, inevitable speed. Bridges and roads are annihilated, and at the Daiichi Nuclear Power Plant three reactors experience level seven meltdowns. From video recordings, a man can be heard screaming, "We've lost everything. Here is like hell on earth."

The lucky few who aren't swallowed up that day climb to the highest points of their roofs waving white flags in a desperate attempt to be rescued. From an aerial view, the flags look like ghosts floating up from doomed bodies, spirits tethered to the flesh in a rush to evacuate.

* * *

As children raised in the evangelical faith, "The Book of Revelation," which prophesies the end of the world, was little more than a bedtime story to my sister and me. To lie on our backs in the tall grass and look at the sky was an act of meditation meant to prepare us for the End Of Times, when jesus would return and bring the whole galaxy crashing down.

In spring, we watched the migratory birds head north for nesting, praying for their safe return along the flyway, between the breeding and wintering grounds.

We read these birds have a neural connection between the eye and the part of the forebrain known as "Cluster N," which becomes active during migration, enabling birds to literally *see* the magnetic field of the earth.

We wanted to go where they could go, see what they could see. We wanted our bodies to be built like their bodies, all mental maps, compass points, instinct, and light.

* * *

J. touched down into our lives one spring like a squall, then stayed on: a foul-smelling fog, a thick marine layer that would not lift.

J. was a hero in town because a cop who was chasing him shot him in the back of the head with a taser and somehow, he ripped it out, hopped a fence, and kept running, managing, that time, to escape.

We were not raised that way, to love boys like him, but she was tangled in him anyway.

Forest for the trees.

* * *

At a very young age, long distance migrant birds go their separate ways, forming strong attachments to potential breeding and wintering sights. Once the attachment is made it is rarely broken—the birds visit the same wintering sites every year.

* * *

In the aftermath of natural disasters like the one in Tōhoku, reports of supernatural experiences increase exponentially.

Five years after the earthquake and tsunami in Tōhoku, Yuka Kudo, a sociology major, began writing her senior thesis on potential supernatural experiences that had taken place in the wake of the disaster. Kudo interviewed one hundred taxi drivers in Ishinomaki, the area that had been hit hardest. Many drivers refused interview, but seven of them reported remarkably similar stories—that of phantom fares. In each instance, a fare entered the cab, requested to be taken to a decimated location, and before reaching their final destination, vanished into thin air.

* * *

"No ghost was ever seen by two sets of eyes," wrote Thomas Carlyle.

* * *

The most frequently cited of Yuko Kudo's studies involves a cab driver in his fifties and the woman who got into his cab near Ishinomaki Station. The woman asked to be taken to the Minamihama district.

"The area is almost empty," the driver said. "Is it okay?"

"Have I died?" the woman replied in a shaking voice.

Perplexed, the driver looked over his shoulder, and found that the woman was gone.

Tōhoku police are now collaborating with local exorcists.

* * *

She says things were good between them in the beginning. That they laughed a lot. That he brought her potent peach blunts and exquisite presents. That he protected her from the harm I sense he is now inflicting. I tell her Heaven is ephemeral. That since Eve and Adam, Paradise has proved unsustainable. That even for far-ranging migratory birds who've made it to the tropics, paradise lasts but a single season.

* * *

When the world breaks apart the way it did in Tōhoku, ghosts rise up to fill the void.

In addition to the phantom fares, firefighters are repeatedly asked to respond to calls from a street that's been washed away by the tidal wave. Mothers report that the toys of their dead children are moving on their own.

Following the Antofagasta landslide in Chile, sobbing and screaming has been ringing through the darkness for decades. A four-year-old boy dressed in white walks through walls and peers in people's windows.

Again in Chile, following the 2010 earthquake, shadows and disembodied screams rise from the bowels of the devastated parts of the city. Shadows can be seen crossing the Cardinal Raúl Silva Henríquez Bridge, and cell phones light up with incoming calls from disembodied voices that never quite connect.

After the 2004 Indian Ocean earthquake and tsunami, locals reported the spirits of wealthy foreigners wandering the shorelines of obliterated beaches, as though in death the metaphor for their lives was laid plain.

One-hundred-and-six years following the 1910 Avalanche in Wellington, WA, reports of a ghostly woman humming and singing, reports of children playing, and screams so eerie they could only rise from the throats of the dead. "A century later," one woman reports, "they're still trying to find their way home."

* * *

I went once to the trailer park where my Sister and J. lived together. The suspiciously expensive leather furniture was littered with liquor bottles and overflowing ashtrays. Dozens of posters were tacked to the walls, meant to disguise the way they'd come to resemble Swiss cheese beneath his fists. She was uncharacteristically quiet, and he stuck to her like a sun-warmed lozenge to a sweater. He used the words "fag" and "homo" over and over, despite my presence. His pit bull ate my leather boot in a single bite.

When I was leaving that night, I told my Sister that if he ever hurt her, I'd drag him onto the front lawn and beat the shit out of him until the grass drank in his blood.

"I love you," my Sister said, and headed back inside. She never so much as mentioned him after that.

* * *

The night following the visit, I dreamt of the *Odyssey*, of Odysseus sailing beyond the dawn to the untouched, sunless edges of the earth. I watched the ghosts in the meadow of Asphodel flit like shadows.

I woke with traces of the river Lethe on my tongue, remembering that to drink there was to be stripped of one's identity.

* * *

Sometimes a boy is not a boy at all. He is only a convenient way to disappear.

* * *

Despite what sophisticated navigators they are built to be, there are times when migrating birds lose their way. They fly past their destination in the spring overshoot, ending up too far north. Or in the case of reverse migration, a young bird's genetic programming fails, and they end up as stranded vagrants thousands of miles out of range. Or in drift migration, when birds are simply blown off course. Or in abmigration, wherein birds from one region join those from another and end up migrating back, immersed in their new population.

* * *

In many cultures, birds are seen as harbingers of death. They steal souls from the dying, embody spirits of the dead, or act as psychopomps, shepherding souls of the departed from this world to whatever comes next.

* * *

Sparrows, for instance, are built slight and hollow of bone so they may carry home lost spirits of the dead.

Sisters are similarly made so that whomever is lost may live on in the other one lightly.

* * *

Many experts have tried their hand at explaining supernatural phenomena that follows disaster.

Theology Professor Hugo Zepeda claims that the psychological damage suffered by survivors of a single tragedy is so similar that they achieve a "collective projection, which means that they feel or see more or less the same things."

"The perceiver [of ghosts] is prepared for the experience on the basis of his or her having, so to speak, been eaten by pests. The condition is one of eroded defenses, of vulnerability," Elizabeth Robinson writes.

* * *

Some people believe ghosts roam the earth because of unfinished business. Others believe they remain because we are unable to let them go.

* * *

I am hoping this boy is a broken mirror I can bury by moonlight.

I am hoping my sister knows that the story of migration is a story imbued with the hope of returning, and because of that, I will lie in the tall grass between the wintering and breeding grounds. I will pray, in my own way, for her safe return. And always, always, I will watch for her.

LADIES LAZARUS

Mother's eyes are different colors, one brown one green: heterochromia iridum. It is rumored that with such eyes, a person is able to simultaneously perceive two separate planes of being.

You move two thousand miles from the town where you were born, but return each time Mother goes missing.

* * *

What you learned from Mother—the world is full of secret haunts. Places where people go to hide, to become hidden things. One such place is City 40, a closed city constructed around Mayak, the birthplace of the Soviet Union's foremost thermonuclear warhead plant. When those recruited to Mayak moved to City 40 with their families, the border was sealed for eight years, leaving those on the outside to believe their loved ones were dead or disappeared.

* * *

On nights Mother goes missing, you, your Father, and Sister part the marsh, or else move like dull blades through the wood's terrifying sameness. You leave secret notes in the limbs of sugar maples and evergreens.

Please Mother, make yourself known to me.

With Mother, love's an animal trap. Catch and release.

* * *

The dream of City 40 was that of living wages, low crime-rates, and occasional luxuries. A place where children could fish, swim, and play unaccompanied late into the evening. If the price of that dream was a kind of sectioning off from the world, so be it. The trouble, in the end, was not the isolation of City 40. It was the toxicity of the place itself and, once that toxicity was known, the expectation of silence.

* * *

Nights without stars, you walk barefoot across the street and down the hill, along the lake's perimeter. Through the smacking of cattails and itching of Queen Anne's Lace, in this place where plumes of crack smoke are known to curl over the water, you smell her. In the dark, Mother's eyes shine as lakes named for the drowned might.

You know what Mother's doing but don't dare speak it aloud. Rather, you evolve as necessary. A reluctant teleology emerges wherein night vision, telepathy, and thick skin become extrinsic. There is pain there, but you're not allowed to name it.

* * *

When a place is by its very definition secret, misinformation is inevitable. Even the Soviet Union's most ingenious atom-splitters scooped plutonium from the floor with bare hands.

Carelessly, the chemical byproducts of Mayak were discharged into City 40's scenic rivers, and once the radioactivity made its way north to the Arctic Ocean, and was traced back to a single point of origin, their secret was out. The central water supply of City 40 was permanently poisoned, its lakes and rivers known as "graveyards of the earth."

* * *

Mother and Father planted roots in a town where no one leaves. The kind of place that makes one feel as though one is fated to it. In such towns, one must become creative if one is to escape.

For Mother, two worlds—earth you inhabit together, then the hot, heavenly body of euphoria and speed. Often,

Mother exists in the tear between these worlds, belonging nowhere, to no one.

Everyone sees clearly what she cannot—that her sickness and relief are cyclical now.

* * *

It wasn't until 1994 that the closed status of City 40 was lifted, and those who'd been dreaming of rising from Mayak's ashes were permitted to do so, though at great personal cost. The fact that nearly everyone remained in City 40 behind that border of razorwire had less to do with civic pride, safety, or luxury, and more to do with the fact that City 40 was all they'd ever known.

* * *

There are places in the city only you will go to look for Mother.
Singed brick, dogs on choke chains, weedy lots.

At some point, every woman in town has overdosed, come back from the dead. Ladies Lazarus in a sunless subdivision.

The only cure is not to take the medicine.

Mother's eyes are different colors, and you are the inheritor of the dark eye, the brown-eyed daughter.

* * *

Once you've moved away, Mother mails you a slender manila envelope each week. Inside are seven clippings—your daily horoscopes, as you and Mother are the same sign.

These horoscopes, lifted from the *National Enquirer*, are always strangely specific:

Beware a woman in a green sweater on a red bicycle.

A bearded man in a fedora will reveal a path to great wealth.

Initially, you watch with vigilance for the people described. As time goes by, you imagine them as residents of a closed city where everyone's whereabouts are known, a city that could belong only to Mother and to you.

* * *

I should live in salt, a song on the radio says, *for leaving you.*[1]

* * *

You quit smoking. Start again. Lose yourself in a heroin summer, then for years remain clean, ascetic. In your family and your town, addiction is inherited, toxicity's a birthright, so you test the limits, seeking proof that no matter how close

---

1 The National, "I Should Live in Salt"

you come to failing, you'll competently navigate earth and heaven, never catching in the space between.

* * *

When thinking of Lazarus, we recall the miracle. A man who rose from the dead into waking life. What we forget about the story is how it began. How jesus was aware of Lazarus's illness, but waited until he'd been entombed for four days before doing anything about it. When before a throng of people, jesus wept, declaring, "Whosoever liveth and believeth in me shall never die," and when he ordered the stone rolled away from the tomb, and Lazarus stepped into the sunlight still wrapped in his grave-cloths, that had nothing to do with Lazarus, with healing or miracles. That was jesus showing the people of Bethany his power, nothing more.

* * *

There are over eighty-thousand people who remain in City 40, now known as Ozersk. Eighty-thousand closely guarded secrets.

This morning in Ozersk, cattle will come to drink from the riverbed. They will stir up the radionuclide sediment at the bottom that everyone wants to forget until it mixes with the clear water at the river's surface. Radioactivity will seep into the milk, and that milk will be made for raw consumption.

* * *

You are facing the fact that Mother is unknowable, that parts of Mother which rocked shut will never be open to you again. You lay on your back in the hollows of what you know of Mother and try to soak it in. But there is little floating room between rock bottom and bone.

When the sun is closest to the horizon, you'll comb the marsh for Mother's shadow, remembering how when you were small, you'd walk at a pace that allowed your shadow to be absorbed within Mother's. As though through this small action you might somehow be reabsorbed. As though through such synthesized darkness, the two of you might somehow become indistinguishable from one another.

Some nights, you're certain you see bright hair among the lily pads.

EPISTLE FOR SUICIDED MOTHERS

Mother Teasdale,

Between the lifeline and the mercury line, the pills are smooth and round. How strange that what fits in a palm should kill you. That it can, that it does. In the tub, in the warm water, your skin takes on that pinking pallor, a final blush so beautiful it culls your former suitor from the dead. Drinker of poison, he will ask again for your hand. Do not offer it. Do not follow him to the dark place.

Spring again. Swallows circle, frogs in pools sing, the wild plum trees whistle, all these things remind us of you.

Mother Woolf,

By the edge of the river you laid your walking stick down. Later they would find it there, beside your footprints, and hope against all evidence you'd wandered off. On the contrary, you were quite measured. Two deceased parents, two more years of insanity, two of war. Weight of stones. Force of current. Like every sentence penned, your death was perfect.

Between Blitzkrieg and the voices, you wanted quiet. Where better than underwater, where all you can hear is your heart?

If I could, I would reach in the River Ouse and pull you to shore by your hair. But I can't, and when *I* break down, *yours* is the voice I hear.

Mother Sexton,

You write in June of bats beating in the trees like a woman who's been hovered over. Parents, descendants, healers and lovers betrayed you. You'll be dead by October. So much talk of your lipsticks and furs, your flirtations, the manner of your lover's knots. Even your want to die is called "a lust." Even your ignition described as "turned on." I'll hear on more than one occasion how on the afternoon of your death, you came home and removed your rings. As though, after confessional poetry and private transcripts released by your analyst, they needed new ways to make you bare.

If I were you, I'd have sealed the garage too, just to be alone with the radio.

Mother Plath,

Think of my body as your favorite haunt, and enter. I am more than happy to host. Winter evenings are shaped like your crawl space. Mornings, the oven hums like your father's hives. I've called you via Ouija, and more than once taken the train from London to Heptonstall to leave my lipstick on your grave. Your daughter, with her dowry of milk and bread, writes of the way you are "up-dug / for repeat performances", but it is not your head upon the rack that makes you Patron Saint of anything.

It is the way that even now, you rise.

THE SYLVIA PLATH EFFECT

> What should I do with my mind? Think
> of the way it broke until the breaking is
> language.
>
> —ALLISON BENIS WHITE

The romantic link between madness and genius is an ancient one that dates back at least as far as Aristotle's musings
on "melancholia." There are many factors, both believed and
empirical, that support this theory or, if you will, this romance.
Among the most commonly cited: the mentally ill experience
and are thus able to convey an extraordinary intensity of feeling, and are able to experience the world uniquely, in ways the
mentally "well" could never imagine. Consider, for instance,
Einstein's radical approach to theoretical physics, or the way
Van Gogh's *Starry Night* elevated painting beyond mere rep-
resentation of the physical world.

Following a series of interesting but insufficient psychological studies regarding potential links between creativity and mental illness, psychologist James C. Kaufman published a new study in the *Review of General Psychology* in 2001 concluding that female poets suffered from mental illness in unprecedented disproportion to their male counterparts, as well as to writers of every other genre, and that they were furthermore found to experience significantly more personal tragedy.

Kaufman argued that there were several factors associated with poetry itself that might produce this additive effect. First, that people who are attracted to poetry as an art form are statistically more likely to be mentally unstable. Second, that unlike other art forms, poetry does not "assuage mental illness," as it is not a sufficient form of catharsis. Third, that due to the mythology associated with the life of poets (a mythology, one might argue, that Kaufman himself is helping to perpetuate), poets are not only encouraged, but expected to be mentally ill. Fourth, that poets tend to peak at a young age when mental illness is most likely to manifest.

Kaufman's study, with its shocking lack of nuance not only toward mental illness and the artistic process but also, unsurprisingly, toward women, further cites, "the greater difficulty that women tend to experience in ignoring extrinsic motivational constraints." As though historically, ignoring such constraints would have even been possible.

Capitalizing on the name of "one of the most gifted and troubled poets in the sample," James C. Kaufman titled his early finding "The Sylvia Plath Effect."

* * *

As is the case with many infamous figures, Sylvia Plath's work is almost impossible to evaluate when it is stripped completely of personal context. Hers is one of the most infamous suicides in literary history, and this both shapes and mars the essence of her genius.

The novice poets who most admire Plath do belong to a kind of cult. They gather together in the Church Of Holy Intensity. They are tattooed with quotes, or fleshy replicas of her pen and ink drawings. They defend her vehemently, against criticism and history and her husband, Ted Hughes, whom many believe was the single most significant factor in her death. At some point, Plath's grave in Heptonstall had to be moved, because so-called feminists came from all over the world to eradicate her married surname from her tombstone. Plath devotees are a passionate bunch, but every famous writer has devoted readers. What is perhaps most fascinating about Plath, a mentally ill woman who was abandoned by her husband and forced to undergo electroconvulsive therapy before killing herself at the age of thirty, is that so often, her fans transition from loving her to wanting to be her.

I myself was guilty of this as a young writer and—full disclosure—I believe that I am guilty of it now. As a kind of creative but deeply bipolar teenager in a less than literary town, what I wanted more than anything was to achieve creative transmigration. I laid my own glib, sophomoric work overtop Plath's as though it were tracing paper. The result was that the most obvious traits of Plath's came through, but all that was beautiful, original, fierce, or nuanced in her writing transferred very crudely into my own.

When I first came in contact with *Ariel*, I remember thinking, this is what it feels like to be penetrated. This is what it means to be consumed, to be in love.

Like a slowly leaking poison, Plath has a way of turning young readers and writers into sycophants. But why? Is it the power of her work that draws us in, or is it the strange and brutal mythology surrounding her life and death?

* * *

In the opening stanza of her poem, "My Mother," Sylvia Plath's daughter, Frieda, writes:

> They are killing her again.
> She said she did it
> One year in every ten,
> But they do it annually, or weekly,
> Some even do it daily,
> Carrying her death around in their heads
> And practising it. She saves them
> The trouble of their own;
> They can die through her
> Without ever making
> The decision. My buried mother
> Is up-dug for repeat performances.

Frieda's uncanny battle cry of a poem takes no prisoners when it comes to a certain kind of Plath devotee. Frieda is not wrong in her assertion that these people exist, that in fact, they are everywhere. There is an enormous faction of people who falsely romanticize mental illness, not only, but particularly, where Plath is concerned. In my opinion, these people tend to be sad, troubled, or bored more often than they are actually mentally ill.

I do think that the artist's struggle when it comes to mental illness is that, within the realm of inspiration, they are seen as possessing some special, potentially unfair advantage while, in their daily lives, the same mental illness is seen as the ultimate handicap that will almost certainly prevent them from thriving.

The truth lies, most likely, in some amalgam of this juxtaposition. To be certain, the balance is delicate.

On the one hand, the assumption that struggle prevents success, that mental illness is by its very nature prohibitive, particularly in writing where a book must be, as Kafka would say "an axe for the frozen sea within us," this is reductive, it is foolish, and harmful to writers with mood disorders who have no choice but to thrive.

On the other hand, one of the reasons why allegedly scientific findings such as James C. Kaufman's "Sylvia Plath Effect," are damaging is that they seem to suggest that mental illness is an artistic leg up on everyone else, when nothing could be further from the truth. That mentally ill people are blessed with creativity and intensity may very well be true, but the evenness and sustained concentration it takes to create with masterful precision is in direct and often disheartening contrast to the depressive or bipolar temperament.

Depending upon which world you're moving through, mental illness will be seen as a superpower or a disability.

But suicidal ideation is another thing altogether.

In the words of the great Fran Lebowitz, "If you are of the opinion that the contemplation of suicide is sufficient evidence of a poetic nature, do not forget that actions speak louder than words."

* * *

During one of my worst psychotic breaks, I believed that Sylvia Plath had come back from the dead as a dybbuk who lived inside me. It began when, unable to sleep at night, I envisioned our bodies side by side in the cold soil of the crawl space where she first attempted suicide. The only time I felt peace was there in that blistering darkness, the two of us emptied of all our furtive confessions. In time, that meditation became, in my mind, a granted wish. Sylvia came to live inside me, though it wasn't something I could control. Initially I was happy to be haunted by my heroine, but often, she was cruel to me. She curled around me, shook the bed at night, tittered wetly in my ear with her oven-hot breath.

Frightened, I asked her to leave, but she refused. Every time I looked in the mirror, I'd see a flash of her golden hair superimposed. Sometimes I'd walk at night and the sky would be a-swarm with bees. At the worst point of that psychotic break, I heard screaming when I turned the oven knobs, and screaming every time I poured the milk.

Researchers in the field of anomalistic psychology explain poltergeist activity as the result of illusion, lapses in memory, and wishful thinking. Which doesn't answer the question of why, if you could wish for anything, it would be the presence of a poltergeist inside.

* * *

To those who are not readers of Sylvia Plath's work, she is simply a poster girl for suicide. After all, she wrote about it constantly. And yes, she attempted it at least three times. So infamously suicidal was she that most people believe that final attempt was the fulfillment of her ultimate wish. But those close to Plath claim the last attempt was most likely an accident, a kind of ritualistic cry for help that she was used to surviving. We'll never know whether she meant to die, or if, for some strange reason, every possible element conspired against her.

A. Alvarez writes:

> It was a mistake, then, and out of it a whole myth has grown. I don't think she would have found it much to her taste, since it is a myth of the poet as a sacrificial victim... In these terms, her suicide becomes the whole point of

the story, the act which validates her poems, gives them their interest and proves her seriousness… Yet just as the suicide adds nothing at all to the poetry, so the myth of Sylvia as a passive victim is a total perversion of the woman she was… Above all, it misses the courage with which she was able to turn disaster into art.

* * *

From a practical standpoint, a successful suicide attempt is, of course, the antithesis of creation. But to burn with the question of life, of whether it is worth living, is a philosophical sojourn that everyone, at some point, must enter into. Because a known consequence of mood disorders is suicide (the risk estimated at at least twenty percent), artists who live with this condition are uniquely qualified to examine and perhaps even assist in answering this question for all of us.

"In (her poems)," writes Alvarez, "she faced her private horrors steadily and without looking aside, but the effort and risk involved in doing so acted on her like a stimulant: the worse things got and the more directly she wrote about them, the more fertile her imagination became."

This depiction of Plath's creative process describes an object in motion that had no choice but to stay in motion. It is a kind of horror story for writers—that the meaningful thing that keeps you alive is capable of killing you to achieve its own end.

"The question," wrote Emerson, "is whether suicide is the way out or the way in."

I'd like to think for Plath, it was both, or, better yet, that it was neither. That she was so in tune with worlds we cannot imagine that she was unable to take seriously the thin scrim that separated daily life from a permanent place in the ground.

In her poem, "Lady Lazarus," she writes:

> Dying
> Is an art, like everything else.
> I do it exceptionally well.
>
> I do it so it feels like hell.
> I do it so it feels real.
> I guess you could say I've a call.

The overwhelming sentiment of the poem is that for Plath, death and resurrection are magic tricks of a kind. But read in a certain light, she's also describing suicide as a tool, a kind of double lens through which poetry is created, and through which, for her readers, that poetry is felt, interpreted, and seen.

Alvarez: "The authority of her poetry was in part due to her brave persistence in following the thread of her inspiration right down to the Minotaur's lair."

There are those who believe that to visit the Minotaur's lair means never to come back up, though having lived with the relentless ups and downs of manic-depression, I doubt that was the belief of Plath herself. I myself am not convinced that her work necessitated death, or that she contributed all she might have to poetry and to the world.

As to the question of whether *Ariel* was worth its human sacrifice, if that was indeed what happened, I am ashamed that I don't have a kinder, more empathic answer for that.

* * *

It is curious to me that someone as creatively brilliant and formally rigorous as Plath is sometimes considered to be a lesser poet. Perhaps it's because her novel, *The Bell Jar*, reads to certain naysayers as juvenilia. Perhaps in the minds of some, the legendary quality of her life undercuts the ultimate seriousness and worth of her work. Perhaps it is her followers, who meet in the Church Of Holy Intensity, and compose their pastiche poetry, turning her legacy into an emo affair. In my experience, it is not that her work is vulnerable, or frightening, and it is not that she was mentally ill. The suggestion that Plath was "lesser" seems to have more to do with the fact that her work is potently, unapologetically female.

Maggie Nelson writes:

> A woman who explores the depths of her despair or depression isn't typically valorized as a hero on a fearless quest to render "darkness visible," but is instead perceived as a redundant example of female vulnerability, fragility, or self-destructiveness. A woman who lives...like a mad animal at the furthest reaches of her sanity isn't a shamanistic voyager to the dark side, but a 'madwoman in the attic,' an abject spectacle.

The perceived limitations of gender were a theme not only in Plath's work, but too in her life. It is reported that, in great pain, Plath asked her psychiatrist for a lobotomy. He laughed at her and said, "You're not going to get off that easy."

* * *

It is possible we would know far more about Plath, her motivations and plans for future work, if her husband, Ted Hughes, and Assia Wevil, his mistress-turned-second-wife, had not destroyed new works in the wake of her death. Purportedly, there was a novel, and a journal, which Ted claimed he demolished because he didn't want his children ever to read it. Recently, letters that Plath mailed to her American psychiatrist have emerged, alleging that Hughes beat her two days prior to her miscarrying a child, and also that he wanted her dead.

Short of this new correspondence emerging, Wevil's account of Plath's final works is the sole affidavit of their content.

It is also possible, though I doubt it, that those grave-defacing feminists are right, and Ted Hughes possessed a crude kind of voodoo. Descriptions of him include "nature poet," "laureate," "sexual predator," "philanderer," and my personal favorite, "in bed, he smelled like a butcher" (courtesy of Assia Wevil herself). Both of his wives killed themselves in exactly the same fashion, through gas inhalation. For Hughes' second wife, who managed to escape the Nazis at the beginning of

World War Two, it seemed a peculiar choice, especially considering she took their young child along with her. Add to the pile that later in his life, Ted and Sylvia's son, Nicholas, also committed suicide, and there is no denying the family's tragic pattern, or the impactful manner with which mental illness and suicidal ideation crept down, spider-like, from the branches of the family tree.

* * *

In her poem, "Elm," Plath famously writes:

> I know the bottom, she says. I know it with my great
>   tap root:
> It is what you fear.
> I do not fear it: I have been there.

And yet, in the more conversational, candid atmosphere of her journal, she writes:

> You fool, you are afraid of being alone with your own mind. You just better learn to know yourself, to make decisions before it is too late. […] Stop thinking selfishly of razors & self-wounds & going out and ending it all. Your room is not your prison. […] No one has the power to cure you but yourself.

There is something to this combination of self-aggrandizement and self-hatred, this heady mix of unshakable confidence, self-effacement, and doom. It is not in any single revelation, but in the antithetical combination, where her deepest vulnerabilities lie.

There is also something to the intensity of Plath's "cure." This is something that many people with mood disorders believe, that they can cure themselves. Given the advancements in pharmaceutical treatment for mental health, this idea is less pervasive than it used to be. At the time Plath was alive, she was positioned somewhere between the medieval practice of holes drilled in the skull to drain the demons and that tired epithet about pulling yourself up by your bootstraps. It is untrue that someone suffering from manic depression can cure herself through sheer will; however, when the desperation to be cured is manifested through works of art, that work has the potential to be unbelievably compelling. Think how intense, how rapt the world would be if, embedded in everyone's profession, were the high stakes of grappling with life and death.

* * *

The most beautiful point of connection *I* have to Plath is not her mental illness, or even her poetry. Certainly it is not the juicy details of the literary soap opera her life became. Her work, unmatched in its ingenious, unapologetic intensity, could only have been created by Plath and Plath alone, and I do not believe that mental illness provided her with any particular advantage, at least not in a way that did not balance out.

What I love about her work is its hopefulness for a person like me.

To know that not so far away and not so long ago, a woman with my diagnosis, familiar with the anguish and ugliness endemic to such a life, was able to use it also as a filter for beauty.

That the sins she committed because of said illness were used not as a measure of shame but rather, repurposed as a mode of connection, embraced as a literary gift.

To see manifested in her work that all of the pain and the struggle is useful, that it comes to something, that is the single most important gift anyone has ever given me.

* * *

To be imbued with the unshakeable belief that life is to be lived in service of art.

To know the necessity of loneliness in order to illuminate and assuage it for others.

To understand that every rejection letter is a gift, humiliation is a church and poverty a proficiency.

That being nine-lived has little to do with luck and everything to do with getting back up again.

To carry a lantern into hell in order to say with certainty what the light is like.

To let god and the devil move through you in equal measure.

To allow nothing, no symptom, no mood nor its resulting tortures, to come between you and the page.

To soak up every syllable and caesura of the authors who move you.

To devote your life to craft with the evangelical fervor of someone who is born again.

These combined are the characteristics that make up a writer, and embracing the privilege and the beauty of such a life with your every atom, *that* is truly the Sylvia Plath Effect.

THE MOON, FROM THE BITTER COLD OF OUTER SPACE, CROONS TO THE GRIDDLE OF THE DESERT[5]

If the world was yours, the first thing you would do is make me disappear.

So I save you the trouble.

As I leave Seattle in the rearview, I mourn the smell of fecund moss, the feeling of the Sound's briny breath upon me. Already I am aching for cherry blossoms and pretentious coffee, for bookstores that served as bright and sacred churches.

"I understand pilgrimage," writes Jericho Parms, "as an act that asks the body to journey for the soul. To summit a mountain, to complete a trail, to reach an ancient monument offers a tangible sense of arrival. The worn and weary legs of a pilgrim are but a physical expression."

---

5 C.D. Wright

I tell myself that I am a pilgrim, body blazing through sublime pastoral toward the dream of home, but can you call yourself a pilgrim if your central motivation is to flee?

Is this pilgrimage, or exile?

Perhaps these are not useful questions.

* * *

Seneca: *Let us train our minds to desire what the situation demands.*

* * *

For two thousand miles, I chain-smoke in my duct-taped zip-tied Toyota.

At the halfway point of my journey, somewhere in the middle of Utah, there are horses, cows, and tiny Mormon towns I'm too scared to stop in. At one point, something amazing happens—that rare moment in which you can see the exact place the rain begins, falling in a single sheet. I know it isn't for you, but I love being the inhabitor of two simultaneous worlds.

I feel most like myself at twilight, gazing through breaks in the high clouds where sunlight seeps through. Crepuscular rays—your wife taught me the name. God clouds is what my mother always calls them.

The worst part of the drive is when, for a long stretch, there is nothing but one lone tree. I feel that tree is a metaphor for my everything, or else that I am doomed to become that tree the moment I die and am reborn.

* * *

Forgive me. I was trying to save you the trouble of getting rid of me and now I've gone and explained at length what it was like to depart.

The point is, I live in the Arizona desert now.

It would be lonely here, but for spring, the rooftops all tangled in jasmine. The sidewalks littered with burst lemons, freeways lined with lush bougainvillea blossoms the color of a freshly blotted kiss. It rarely rains here, never like where you are, and even in the middle of the night, I can hear the interlaced arias of birdsong.

As you know, I am in what might be referred to as failing mental health. When mood disorder symptoms and trauma symptoms collide, I experience that special kind of agony where I can feel my eyelashes writhing.

Is this something you've experienced?

One way I'm coping is by smoking too much, a ritual, which exacerbates the very thing I seek to relieve. You see, the man who raped me chain-smoked Marlboros, and his tongue tasted of something rotten covered in honey. In an attempt to calm my nerves, I inhale, and in doing so, exhale what feels like another forced kiss.

*　*　*

It must seem like paradise now: that small window of time in which I was nothing to you but a vague story, a half-kept secret.

*　*　*

Your wife says I'm always running from something—fair, considering all the times we've crammed my belongings into trash bags and lowered them, like bodies, into my trunk in the middle of the night. But I disagree. I prefer to think of my life and my body as a moveable feast. To shore against ephemera, I erect an altar wherever I go, lying carefully upon it small gifts that hold great meaning for me. I've found that a traveling altar makes more sense for my life than a stable home. The purpose of a home, after all, is shelter, something I am not sure I desire, or deserve. The purpose of an altar is to dissolve boundaries, separating sanctum from street, sacred from profane. An altar might not be a roof, but it will not catch me like a rat trap either.

*　*　*

It once was the case that all of life, down to the most quotidian of deeds, served both practical and spiritual purposes. Working, eating, and sex, were functional, and also a sacrament, an opportunity to commune with what is holy.

It is said that in the modern world, we have abandoned this communion, that our daily lives are desacralized, profane and, as such, we move through the world drained and disillusioned.

* * *

Naturalist John Muir believed he could speak to god by communing with the wilderness. His rituals of communion included scaling enormous trees as they were ripped apart by twisters and moving swiftly between rapidly shifting glaciers.

I am jealous of men, of their freedom, and the likelihood they will die not of violence, but of misadventure.

* * *

Deus absconditus: hidden god. Remote god who ignores human suffering.

* * *

Shortly before I met your wife, I was assaulted one night on a deserted beach. That I am writing you now is a miracle, an uneasy miracle considering all the women who have not shared my good fortune. Driving home that night, weighing my luck against my body's ruin, I made a decision: my then-partner could never know.

I feared she would blame me, chastise my poor choices, insinuate that maybe I'd wanted a man all along. I was worried she would hold my body the way she once did a kamikaze bird's that'd smashed against the grill of our car on the freeway. I felt certain she would touch me less, *even less*, if that were possible. I couldn't risk those things, as any one of them would be enough to break me. So I stayed quiet. Covered my body, created an alibi, and spent the next few weeks barely daring to breathe.

It is not her fault that I hid when all I wanted was for someone to really see me. To cradle me so close to their chest that their heart sounded in the empty socket of my own. To say, upon seeing the sucked wounds of my body, *no man will ever have what it takes to ruin you.* To stroke the teeth marks in my chest and assure me, *yes, you are cratered now, but so, my love, is the moon.*

I also had to consider that like every woman I've ever known, my partner came to me, some part of her still held down, some man's fingerprints still ghosting across her throat. One afternoon, she showed me a journal she kept just after it happened—hundreds of drawings of the clock she stared at as she turned blue and every soft thing about her was brutalized. To think that such a trigger exists—the ticking of time itself. What I wanted, more than anything, was to make a soft, beautiful cocoon for her to live inside. Part of that meant understanding that every time I reached for her, I risked the vivid resurfacing of the original violence.

* * *

> Eliade argued that all rituals at their core are reenactments of the primordial deeds performed by God, gods, or mythical ancestors during the period of creation. In imitating the gods, it is as if the original events are happening once more, and the ritual releases some of the potent, transformative power that was present at the very beginning of the world.[6]

When god created the world, he created a lonely man. Woman was an apology, an afterthought. Woman was a Frankensteinian companion built from a borrowed bone, her breath made of blown dust. In this regard, I need no ritual, potent or otherwise, to remind me of god's primordial deeds. I am acutely aware that in desire, I am an object, in war, a tactic. In our broken friendship, I am hobby or fetish. That's how you refer to me, as though you never learned my name.

* * *

He was playing god when he parked the bike, when he showed me the gun. "Have a seat," god commanded—I could just barely hear him over my heart. We sat there for a moment, him chain-smoking Marlboros, me holding my breath, as though if I were still enough, I'd disappear.

---

6 Brett and Kate McKay

"I'm so sorry I tried to escape," said I, god's humble servant.

God stomped out his cigarette, took my hair gently in his hands and for a moment I could breathe; I could imagine god was merciful. Then his fist tightened, and he dragged me by the hair to a place where no one would find me.

All that night, I appealed desperately to my regularly scheduled Sunday school god. Save me. And fuck a holy trinity; he amounted to nothing more than your average ghost.

Perhaps there was a god who created the heavens and the earth, but that god is dead. In his place, every man who burns the world down for the sheer pleasure of getting away with it.

* * *

"A woman regards her body uneasily," wrote Leonard Cohen, "as though it were an unreliable ally in the battle for love."

This is especially true when the body is reduced to scorched earth.

Every day, I lied to my partner, smothered the urge to be honest.

Sleep did not come easily.

Most nights I stared at the ceiling, every cell in my body whispering what he'd done.

* * *

Despite what you believe, I did not lie to you. I am guilty, at most, of minding my own business.

Perhaps that is not entirely true.

Ocean Vuong writes:

> (h)unger neglects pride
> the way fire
> neglects the cries
> of what it burns

I will confess here that I was hungry for something you thought was yours. That that hunger saved me in ways I could never have imagined. And it is sad but true that fairness, and grace, these are not the burdens of survival.

* * *

From time to time, I sift through the Bildungsromane of our brief relationship—some thirty emails saved in a desktop folder—and hate myself for everything I might have done differently. The tone of the letters is always the same—I defer to you like a frightened dog offering up her belly. I speak of your writerly talents with reverence. For the most part, we avoid the subject of your wife, as though she is the missing letter E in Perec's Oulipo masterpiece. We agree that yes, we both love your wife, but yes, we must co-exist, and yes, jealousy, and yes, fear, are inevitable, but yes, we will be gentle with one another, we will prove that peaceful non-monogamy is possible. And yes, at some point, we use the word "love." I love you. And it feels completely genuine. So when you send me an email at the end of June saying you never want to see or hear from me again, I feel it intensely with my whole body. First, a swift nausea that sours my stomach for weeks. Later, something like a pinched nerve or slipped disc—a short, sharp shock every time I think of you, and every time I finally manage to forget.

* * *

When a man takes on the desecrated body of a woman, there are those who consider him heroic for doing so. He is, through his own gentle existence, redeeming his gender. He touches the female body and in doing so, renders it sacrosanct. Not every man is a rapist—no question. But if he wanted to, any man could get away with rape. And I have yet to meet a woman who moves through the world unscathed by that.

At the end of the day, any man can be Orpheus, killing the underworld softly with his song. A woman, however, must be victim and savior, Euridyce and Orpheus both.

* * *

I kept every present you've given me: three cards, a small magnet in the shape of a rabbit, a lipstick the color of bloodstain which suits me perfectly, but which I now cannot bring myself to apply.

I read recently that in ancient Maya, Kings and Noblemen performed the ritual of cutting themselves open and bleeding deeply into paper bowls. Once the bowls were seeped in blood, they became a papyrus upon which some sacred text would be revealed—a divine vision or a hallowed psalm.

What I want to believe is that you are the King, and the hurtful things you write about me are tied to the ritual of bloodletting. That when the paper is dry, a new vision of me will emerge—one in which I am a human being with a name and a shared desire to peacefully coexist.

* * *

"Every sin is the result of a collaboration," wrote Seneca, and, elsewhere, "Whatever one of us blames in another, each one will find in his own heart."

* * *

There will be no returning to a time in which you loved me. Now I have to become someone I can believe in, someone imbued with something holy, despite the body's Babel. My posture is perfect, my heels so high that I am a tower that nearly reaches heaven. The trouble is, every craving, every wound, has a language all its own. In attempting to trace any one of these languages back to a singular origin, I discover the etymology scorched and scattered, which means that by trying to survive them, the true stories of my body have potentially been lost forever.

* * *

"To keep oneself safe does not mean to bury oneself," wrote Seneca, before he was exiled and forced to commit suicide.

* * *

I hoped that after everything, I'd become fearless.

Each time I leave the house, even for some small errand in the light of day, I am shaking.

Marlboros, motorcycles, heavy metal. The smell of a man. Any man.

And suddenly, I'm back on that beach again.

Pinned against the driftwood.

Remembering how I saw my mother, father, sister, and partner on that beach, their faces rising up from the sand in a cone of light. How the weapon moved, and each of them went out like a match.

So here is my pocketknife with burlesque dancers on the handle whom I call my lovely assistants.

Here is my butterfly knife, wiped clean of the blood of four men.

Here is bejeweled mace I wear like a necklace; here is my illegal lilac-colored taser. Here is my phone, 911 at the ready.

And a lit cigarette to burn with if necessary.

Here are my keys between my fingers.

Here, instructions for escaping a chokehold that I rehearse even as I sleep.

Here and here are the parts of my body no one can touch.

Here is my body, no longer an instrument of touch, but of violence.

* * *

Most of the festivals that celebrate life occur during the height of celestial darkness.

* * *

Three cards, a small magnet in the shape of a rabbit, a lipstick the color of bloodstain which suits me perfectly.

Objects I have lain upon my altar.

Objects I would save from the fire.

* * *

"Love:" wrote Allison Benis White, "To be injured in the same way at the same time."

By this definition, in too many ways to count, this thing between us is love.

* * *

Perhaps I ought to just speak for myself.

I love you still.

Even here, on the receiving end of your thinly veiled roman à clef.

* * *

Six months have passed, and still I feel like a pale alien here—the landscape looming and foreign, something like the surface of Mars. But there are days when I'm driving down Black Canyon Highway with the windows open as wide as they'll go, and my car is pouring music as the sun bears down upon the mountains, and for a moment my ruined body soaks in a small dose of paradise, and I think of you, miserable beneath the April sky where *there is no sunset / just movements inside the light and then a sinking away.*[7]

* * *

Try as we might to remain whole, everything requires a sacrifice. Comfort upon the altar of knowledge, agony upon the altar of love.

* * *

One night your wife and I return to the place where he raped me. I don't know why. Maybe I want something cogent from the mess. Maybe if I swallow the night whole it will

7 Anne Carson

become a singular story, rather than a series of sick and broken flashbacks that wake me in the night.

Your wife saved my life again that night. Held me, though my violent sobbing was enough to break her bones. It was the first and *only* night of my life that I allowed someone to truly see me. Not a girlfriend. Not a hobby or fetish. Not a victim pinned against driftwood on a dark beach who believes she is already dead.

Rather, a woman whose wounds are worth salving.

Whose cratered skin is finally named beautiful.

* * *

Your body told me in a dream it wasn't afraid of anything[8] she said.

I believed her, and I was reborn.

* * *

If the world was yours, the first thing you would do is make me disappear.

You have no idea how close you came to getting what you wanted.

* * *

Quis hic locus?, quae regio?, quae mundi plaga?[9]

What world is this? What kingdom? What shores of what world?

8 Richard Siken
9 T.S. Eliot

* * *

"I've come to understand," Anne Carson writes, "that the best one can hope for as a human is to have a relationship with that emptiness where God would be if God were available, but God isn't."

Did you know this was the space where I kept you once? Roughly where god would be?

Not only because I loved and revered you, but also because I wanted your mercy.

* * *

I understand now that mercy, like fairness, like grace, is not a burden of survival.

* * *

All I know of you now is you are cold, like god is cold, like outer space is.

As for me, I'm doing my best to become the desert whose heat blurs the ether.

So infinite that neither love nor hate can erase me. So inevitable that the wildfires of summer incinerate and still cannot make me disappear.

EPISTLE FOR LOVE AT THE END OF THE WORLD

(1)

I liked it there, in that room with you when, through one small window comes the arcing flood of morning.

I like how morning light is blue.

How time, like blood, is a blue rush.

I like how you said *you are beautiful*, as though it might destroy you.

As though if some part of you isn't anchored inside me, you might very well fly apart.

Among the city's sullied infrastructure, churches burn.

Singed summer nights are flecked with ash.

There is bitterness—the Holy Order no longer grants forgiveness, and the prophesied storm of Seraphim come to save us is but a story now.

We are but a breath from becoming "The Book of Revelation."

If this is the end, I choose your body.

The way your wet against me is holier than a whole kingdom that all through the burning night, sing Hosanna.

(2)

From the dawn of human consciousness, the end of the world has been anxiously anticipated. Now that we know the world will end, and soon, everyone scrambles for salvation.

A cult leader stricken with cancer swears to her followers that if they pray hard enough, they'll resurrect her body from the dead. When at last she succumbs to cancer, her corpse is placed in a coffin beside the pulpit where it remains rotting for six months' time. Journalists catch wind of this, issuing daily reports, which prompts radio personalities to play the song, "Wake up Little Suzie," on repeat. Disgusted and disillusioned with what feels like a devastating joke, many once-devoted followers deem the cult leader a failed Lazarus.

(3)

Longing for quiet, we flock to the center of our once great city.

What used to be the ingenuity of industry is now the architecture of loss.

It is autumn, the cold a suggestion in the ether that eases the brittle sky into analogues of indigo.

We wonder, will there be winter?

(4)

The Arctic sea declines, global sea levels rise, ice sheets shrink, the ocean acidifies. The glacial advance and retreat is no longer caused by changes in the Earth's orbit. The earth-orbiting satellites are disgraced angels that sing what we'd rather not know:

There is no more snow on Mount Killimanjaro.

The planet is besieged with mudslides and monsoons.

The polar bears have drowned.

Remember when the Catholic Church threatened with imprisonment those who claimed the earth revolved around the sun, and was round?

(5)

It used to be we'd walk the dogs through the cemetery every Sunday, preferring the respectful company of the dead.

Now teenagers gather, hoping when the rapture comes they'll witness from the front row the souls of the righteous ascending like thawed wasps from a freshly frozen nest.

Though we know it is coming, no one knows exactly what the rapture will look like.

Most assume a white god whose right hand is a scythe slicing the earth-doomed from the heaven-bound.

(6)

At last, it began with starlings calling through thick sheets of rain, the earth smelling sharply of bougainvillea and bone.

Your body getting lighter all the time, and mine imbued with a landlocked heaviness.

From the time I met you, I feared you'd replace me, that you'd cut a girl-shaped hole in the floor beneath me, then cover and caulk the opening so there'd be no break in the rhythm between your new lover's body and mine.

Just last week, we fought, faces smeared with bourbon and salt.

You fell silent, and I said *Bring on the rapture so long as you ascend and leave me here.*

I had no way of knowing we were moving there slowly, and apart, like the broken trains of dreams.

Any day now, the moon will swell or shrink to a sliver of itself.

And the tides will move, and the earth will turn. And will it be terrible or beautiful to watch as you are swept away?

ACKNOWLEDGEMENTS

Eddy, Nancy, and Sarah Daniels, for profound support, inspiration, and love. Every beautiful thing in my life I owe to you, my family.

The incredible Elizabeth J. Colen, for being Virgil and Beatrice both. Not a breath of work would exist without you.

Gareth Lewis, for introducing me to the writing life and showing me the world.

Julie Haar, for being my first reader and best friend forever.

Virginia and Gordon Busfield and Loretto and Charles Daniels, for making all things possible

Caleb Anderson, for your deft attention to this text and your belief in me.

Sarah Galvin, for showing me the world is full of strange and beautiful magic.

Jessica Jarka, for love, loyalty, and continued inspiration.

T.L. DeVaney, for humor and profound technical support.

Tom Nawrocki, who recognized the essayist in me.

David Lazar, my Father of the Essay. All good works stem from you.

My Corporeal Writing Workshop cohort, for sisterhood and invaluable feedback.

V.S. Atkinson, David Bosworth, Aviya Kushner, Heather McHugh, Ed Roberson, Maya Sonenberg, David Trinidad, Pimone Triplett, Shawn Wong, Kate Zambreno, and everyone at The Port Townsend Writing Conference, for life-changing mentorship.

David Shields, for sharing my obsession and giving me unexpected opportunities to grow.

Jenny Boully, for showing me the kind of writer I want to be and always going to bat for me.

Lidia Yuknavitch, sister misfit, for scholarship, mentorship, and inspiration.

Brian Amolsch, Katie Anderson, Elissa Ball, Jessica Rae Bergamino, Karl Bode, Jennifer McGrath Brock, Kishia Brock, and their girls, Olivia and Grace, Jean Burnet, Mary Anne Carter, Andrew Defever, Rebecca Derminer, Sean DeTore, Doug and Rachel Ebert, Lisa Elliot, Erica

Feldmann, Vicki Grafmiller, Kerri Grant, Jeremy Halinen, Elisa Karbin, Imran Kirkland, Kate Lebo, Lauren Leisse, M.L. Liebler, Kaira Loving, Joseph Massey, Toni Nealie, Jay and Lynn Otlewski, Ryan Pacheco, Deborah Poe, Kristen Radtke, Lisa Ritscher, Dan Rogers, Sheri Rysdam, Christina Santiago, Claire Scott, Jake Uitti, Sarah Vasil, Jennifer Watkins, Jennifer Watman, Arisa White, Elizabeth Yetter, and Maged Zaher, for being the most incredible people on the planet.

The following publications for publishing essays, sometimes in their earlier iterations: *Hotel Amerika*, *The Rumpus*, *The Monarch Review*, *Enclave*, and *Tarpaulin Sky*.

Omar Little Daniels, for being my sweet and wonderful best friend.

Christian Peet, ingenious publisher and cherished friend, for bringing my dreams to fruition.

And to the universe, for so much unexpected beauty and grace.

ABOUT THE AUTHOR

Piper J. Daniels is a Michigan native, queer intersectional feminist, and professional ghostwriter who holds a BA from Columbia College Chicago and an MFA from the University of Washington. She is the co-winner of the 2017 Tarpaulin Sky Book Prize. Her work appears in *Hotel Amerika*, *The Rumpus*, *The Monarch Review*, *WomenArts Quarterly*, *Tarpaulin Sky*, and elsewhere. She lives in Washington State with her dog, Omar Little Daniels.

TARPAULIN SKY PRESS

Warped from one world to another. (*THE NATION*) Somewhere between Artaud and Lars Von Trier. (*VICE*) Hallucinatory ... trance-inducing.... A kind of nut job's notebook.... Breakneck prose harnesses the throbbing pulse of language itself.... Playful, experimental appeal.... Multivalent, genre-bending.... Unrelenting, grotesque beauty. (*PUBLISHERS WEEKLY*) Simultaneously metaphysical and visceral.... Scary, sexual, and intellectually disarming. (*HUFFINGTON POST*) Horrifying and humbling.... (*THE RUMPUS*) Wholly new. (*IOWA REVIEW*) ....only becomes more surreal. (*NPR BOOKS*) The opposite of boring.... An ominous conflagration devouring the bland terrain of conventional realism.... Dangerous language, a murderous kind ... discomfiting, filthy, hilarious, and ecstatic. (*BOOKSLUT*) Creating a zone where elegance and grace can gambol with the just-plain-fucked-up. (*HTML GIANT*) Uncomfortably enjoyable. (*AMERICAN BOOK REVIEW*) Consistently inventive. (*TRIQUARTERLY*) A peculiar, personal music that is at once apart from and very much surrounded by the world. (*VERSE*) A world of wounded voices. (*HYPERALLERGIC*) Futile, sad, and beautiful. (*NEWPAGES*) Inspired and unexpected. Highly recommended. (*AFTER ELLEN*)

MORE FICTION & NONFICTION
FROM TS PRESS >>

STEVEN DUNN
POTTED MEAT

Co-winner, Tarpaulin Sky Book Award
Shortlist, *Granta*'s "Best of Young American Novelists"
Finalist, Colorado Book Award
SPD Fiction Bestseller

Set in a decaying town in West Virginia, Steven Dunn's debut novel, *Potted Meat,* follows a boy into adolescence as he struggles with abuse, poverty, alcoholism, and racial tensions. A meditation on trauma and the ways in which a person might surivive, if not thrive, *Potted Meat* examines the fear, power, and vulnerability of storytelling itself. "101 pages of miniature texts that keep tapping the nails in, over and over, while speaking as clearly and directly as you could ask.... Bone Thugs, underage drinking, alienation, death, love, Bob Ross, dreams of blood.... Flooded with power." **(BLAKE BUTLER, *VICE MAGAZINE*)** "Full of wonder and silence and beauty and strangeness and ugliness and sadness.... This book needs to be read." **(LAIRD HUNT)** "A visceral intervention across the surface of language, simultaneously cutting to its depths, to change the world.... I feel grateful to be alive during the time in which Steven Dunn writes books." **(SELAH SATERSTROM)**

ELIZABETH HALL
I HAVE DEVOTED MY LIFE TO THE CLITORIS

Co-winner, Tarpaulin Sky Book Award
Finalist, Lambda Literary Award for Bisexual Nonfiction
SPD Nonfiction Bestseller

Debut author Elizabeth Hall set out to read everything that has been written about the clitoris. The result is "Freud, terra cotta cunts, hyenas, anatomists, and Acker, mixed with a certain slant of light on a windowsill and a leg thrown open invite us. Bawdy and beautiful." (WENDY C. ORTIZ). "An orgy of information ... rendered with graceful care, delivering in small bites an investigation of the clit that is simultaneously a meditation on the myriad ways in which smallness hides power." (*THE RUMPUS*) "Marvelously researched and sculpted.... bulleted points rat-tat-tatting the patriarchy, strobing with pleasure." (DODIE BELLAMY) "Philosophers and theorists have always asked what the body is—Hall just goes further than the classical ideal of the male body, beyond the woman as a vessel or victim, past genre as gender, to the clitoris. And we should follow her." (*KENYON REVIEW*) "Gorgeous little book about a gorgeous little organ.... The 'tender button' finally gets its due." (JANET SARBANES) "You will learn and laugh .... God this book is glorious." (SUZANNE SCANLON)

AARON APPS
INTERSEX

"Favorite Nonfiction of 2015," Dennis Cooper
SPD Bestseller and Staff Pick

Intersexed author Aaron Apps's hybrid-genre memoir adopts and
upends historical descriptors of hermaphroditic bodies such as
"imposter," "sexual pervert," "freak of nature," and "unfortunate
monstrosity," tracing the author's own monstrous sex as it perversely
intertwines with gender expectations and medical discourse. "Graphic
vignettes involving live alligators, diarrhea in department store
bathrooms, domesticity, dissected animals, and the medicalization
of sex.... Unafraid of failure and therefore willing to employ risk as
a model for confronting violence, living with it, learning from it."
(*AMERICAN BOOK REVIEW*) "I felt this book in the middle of my own
body. Like the best kind of memoir, Apps brings a reader close to an
experience of life that is both 'unattainable' and attentive to 'what will
emerge from things.' In doing so, he has written a book that bursts
from its very frame." (BHANU KAPIL)

Excerpts from *Intersex* were nominated for a Pushcart Prize by
Carolina Quarterly, and appear in *Best American Essays 2014*.

CLAIRE DONATO
BURIAL

A debut novella that slays even seasoned readers. Set in the mind of a narrator who is grieving the loss of her father, who conflates her hotel room with the morgue, and who encounters characters that may not exist, *Burial* is a little story about an immeasurable black hole; an elegy in prose at once lyrical and intelligent, with no small amount of rot and vomit and ghosts. "Poetic, trance-inducing language turns a reckoning with the confusion of mortality into readerly joy at the sensuality of living." (*PUBLISHERS WEEKLY* "BEST SUMMER READS") "A dark, multivalent, genre-bending book.... Unrelenting, grotesque beauty an exhaustive recursive obsession about the unburiability of the dead, and the incomprehensibility of death." (*PUBLISHERS WEEKLY* STARRED REVIEW) "Dense, potent language captures that sense of the unreal that, for a time, pulls people in mourning to feel closer to the dead than the living.... Sartlingly original and effective." (*MINNEAPOLIS STAR-TRIBUNE*) "A grief-dream, an attempt to un-sew pain from experience and to reveal it in language." (*HTML GIANT*) "A full and vibrant illustration of the restless turns of a mind undergoing trauma.... Donato makes and unmakes the world with words, and what is left shimmers with pain and delight." (**BRIAN EVENSON**) "A gorgeous fugue, an unforgettable progression, a telling I cannot shake." (**HEATHER CHRISTLE**) "Claire Donato's assured and poetic debut augurs a promising career." (**BENJAMIN MOSER**)

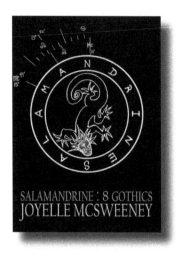

JOYELLE MCSWEENEY
SALAMANDRINE: 8 GOTHICS

Following poet and playwright Joyelle McSweeney's acclaimed novels
Flet, from Fence Books, and *Nylund, The Sarcographer*, from Tarpaulin
Sky Press, comes a collection of shorter prose texts by McSweeney,
Salamandrine: 8 Gothics, perhaps better described as a series of formal/
generic lenses refracting the dread and isolation of contemporary life
and producing a distorted, attenuated, spasmatic experience of time,
as accompanies motherhood. "Vertiginous.... Denying the reader any
orienting poles for the projected reality.... McSweeney's breakneck prose
harnesses the throbbing pulse of language itself." (**PUBLISHERS WEEKLY**)
"Biological, morbid, fanatic, surreal, McSweeney's impulses are to go
to the rhetoric of the maternity mythos by evoking the spooky, sinuous
syntaxes of the gothic and the cleverly constructed political allegory. At
its core is the proposition that writing the mother-body is a viscid cage
match with language and politics in a declining age.... This collection
is the sexy teleological apocrypha of motherhood literature, a siren song
for those mothers 'with no soul to photograph.'" (**THE BROOKLYN RAIL**)
"Language commits incest with itself.... Sounds repeat, replicate, and
mutate in her sentences, monstrous sentences of aural inbreeding and
consangeous consonants, strung out and spinning like the dirtiest
double-helix, dizzy with disease...." (**QUARTERLY WEST**)

JENNY BOULLY
NOT MERELY BECAUSE OF THE UNKNOWN THAT WAS STALKING TOWARD THEM

"This is undoubtedly the contemporary re-treatment that Peter Pan deserves…. Simultaneously metaphysical and visceral, these addresses from Wendy to Peter in lyric prose are scary, sexual, and intellectually disarming." (*HUFFINGTON POST*) In her second SPD Bestseller from Tarpaulin Sky Press, *not merely because of the unknown that was stalking toward them*, Jenny Boully presents a "deliciously creepy" swan song from Wendy Darling to Peter Pan, as Boully reads between the lines of J. M. Barrie's *Peter and Wendy* and emerges with the darker underside, with sinister and subversive places. *not merely because of the unknown* explores, in dreamy and dark prose, how we love, how we pine away, and how we never stop loving and pining away. "To delve into Boully's work is to dive with faith from the plank — to jump, with hope and belief and a wish to see what the author has given us: a fresh, imaginative look at a tale as ageless as Peter himself." (*BOOKSLUT*) "Jenny Boully is a deeply weird writer—in the best way." (*ANDER MONSON*)

MORE FICTION, NONFICTION, POETRY
& HYBRID TEXTS FROM TARPAULIN SKY PRESS

FULL-LENGTH BOOKS

Jenny Boully, *[one love affair]**

Ana Božičević, *Stars of the Night Commute*

Traci O. Connor, *Recipes for Endangered Species*

Mark Cunningham, *Body Language*

Danielle Dutton, *Attempts at a Life*

Sarah Goldstein, *Fables*

Johannes Göransson, *Entrance to a colonial pageant in which we all begin to intricate*

Johannes Göransson, *Haute Surveillance*

Johannes Göransson, *The Sugar Book*

Noah Eli Gordon & Joshua Marie Wilkinson, *Figures for a Darkroom Voice*

Dana Green, *Sometimes the Air in the Room Goes Missing*

Amy King, *The Missing Museum*

Gordon Massman, *The Essential Numbers 1991 - 2008*

Joyelle McSweeney, *Nylund, The Sarcographer*

Kim Parko, *The Grotesque Child*

Joanna Ruocco, *Man's Companions*

Kim Gek Lin Short, *The Bugging Watch & Other Exhibits*

Kim Gek Lin Short, *China Cowboy*

Shelly Taylor, *Black-Eyed Heifer*

Max Winter, *The Pictures*

David Wolach, *Hospitalogy*

Andrew Zornoza, *Where I Stay*

&

Tarpaulin Sky Literary Journal
in print and online

tarpaulinsky.com

CPSIA information can be obtained
at www.ICGtesting.com
Printed in the USA
BVHW082130040319
541742BV00001B/9/P